# DOING
# BUSINESS
## — IN —
# ASIA

# DOING BUSINESS IN ASIA

DAVID L. JAMES

**BETTERWAY BOOKS**
Cincinnati, Ohio

Text maps by Rick Britton
Typography by Park Lane Associates

97 96 95 94 93     5 4 3 2 1

**Library of Congress Cataloging-in-Publication Data**

James, David L., 1933-
    Doing business in Asia : a small business guide to success in
the world's most dynamic market / David L. James.
        p. cm.
    Includes bibliographical references and index.
    ISBN 1-55870-295-4 : $18.95
    1. United States--Commerce--East Asia. 2. East Asia--
Commerce--United States. 3. United States--Commerce--Asia,
Southeastern. 4. Asia, Southeastern--Commerce--Asia. 5.
Marketing--East Asia. 6. Marketing--Asia, Southeastern. I. Title.
HF3126.5.J36 1993
658.8'48'095--dc20                                    92-35271
                                                          CIP

# Acknowledgments

*Doing Business in Asia* is the end product of a series of seminars organized in 1991 by the author, David L. James, and the East-West Center. The seminars were supported in part by the U.S. Small Business Administration under Cooperative Agreement No. SB-IT-90003-01.

The East-West Center, located in Honolulu, Hawaii, is a public, non-profit education and research institution with an international board of governors. The United States Congress established the Center in 1960 with a mandate "to promote better relations and understanding between the United States and the nations of Asia and the Pacific through cooperative study, training, and research." Some 2,000 scholars, government and business leaders, educators, journalists and other professionals annually work with the Center's staff on major Asia-Pacific issues. Since 1960 some 28,000 men and women from the region have participated in the Center's cooperative programs.

The author is grateful to many friends and colleagues—and especially to his wife, Sheila—for their helpful suggestions and comments during the preparation of this guide. However, the opinions, findings, conclusions, and recommendations contained in the guide are those of the author and do not necessarily reflect the views of others, the U.S. Small Business Administration, or the East-West Center.

# PREFACE

This guide has been written primarily for executives and owners of small to medium-sized American businesses who are ready to take the initial steps in marketing their firms' products and services in the most dynamic and challenging economies of the world—the countries and city states of East Asia and Southeast Asia. The guide is also for business people in organizations of all sizes throughout the world who view the earth as a single, accessible marketplace and who are beginning to assess their expanding opportunities in Asia.

Ten countries and city states are the focus of this guide: Japan, China, the "Four Tigers" (Hong Kong, Singapore, South Korea, and Taiwan), and four Southeast Asian nations (Indonesia, Malaysia, the Philippines, and Thailand). Taken as a group, their economies are growing at twice the rate of the rest of the world.

These ten countries are not merely the source of a broad range of products and services that are competing successfully in United States markets, they are markets themselves; markets that are growing rapidly in size, breadth, and sophistication. They cannot be ignored by any American businessman who expects to build a balanced future for himself in today's global economy.

Readers of this guide will gain valuable understanding of the key factors involved in doing business successfully in Asia. They also will find a wealth of practical guidance and useful information, as well as a comprehensive resource section (including a detailed bibliography).

# Contents

## PART I

## PART II

# PART I

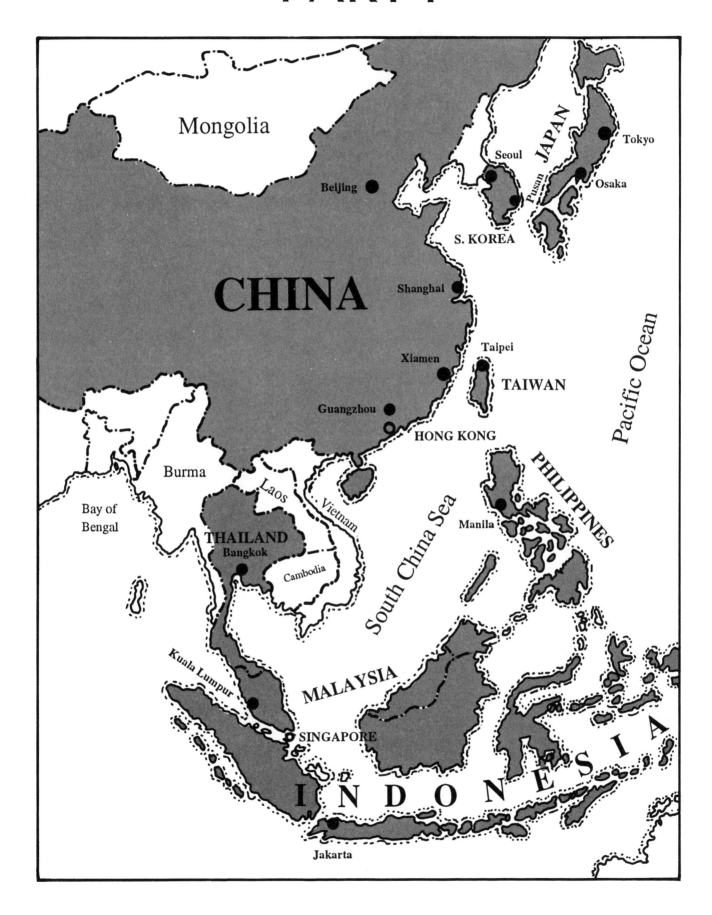

# Chapter 1

# An Asian Tsunami

**ECONOMIC BOOM**

The economic boom in Asia is something like a *tsunami*, the Japanese word for a large tidal wave. A *tsunami* gathers size and momentum from a number of collective forces. Japan's economic strength is the principal force, the one that motivates, activates, and drives forces elsewhere in the region.

Economic success in Asia works like the V-formation of geese in flight. The lead goose is the strongest flyer. It pierces the air head-on and starts an aerodynamic chain that progressively lessens wind resistance for each goose down the line. As the first goose tires, it drops to the rear, and the next goose takes the lead. The analogy to the Asian countries is that Japan's success provides an economic environment that stimulates other economies in the region. As Japan's economy matures, and its rate of growth diminishes, the economy of another country might someday overtake it and assume the lead. South Korea, Taiwan, and even China are presently candidates for the lead position.

The economic development of one country spills over to others in the region. Standards of living and wage rates rise in the successful country. In order to remain competitive, businesses in this country seek lower cost production elsewhere. Japanese capital, for example, has been invested increasingly in offshore production facilities. Japan is now the principal foreign investor in Southeast Asia. Through 1989, its cumulative direct foreign investment in the ASEAN countries (the Association of Southeast Asian Nations—Indonesia, Malaysia, the Philippines, Singapore, Thailand, and Brunei) exceeded $23 billion. Companies like Hitachi, Matsushita, Mitsubishi, and Toyota have expanded their operations in these countries significantly, lowering their production costs and putting them closer to expanding markets.

**Steady Gains for Developing Countries**

As a result of these factors, developing countries in the region have gained strength steadily in recent years. Countries like Indonesia, Malaysia, and Thailand have increased their domestic production of imported products such as rice and various manufactured goods (a process called import substitution) and expanded their exports. Indonesia, for example, now has a $4 billion trade surplus and is on a developmental express train, moving as quickly as it can from a subsistence and resources exporting economy to a value-added industrial economy.

Growth throughout Asia is increasingly technology-driven. Governments in the region are betting that technological innovation is the key to sustained economic development. Consequently, a number of Asian countries—notably Japan, South Korea, Taiwan, and Singapore—are becoming world leaders in technology development. In addition, businesses throughout Asia are, aggressively and opportunistically, expanding their technological capabilities through licensing arrangements, joint ventures, and strategic alliances with American and European firms.

With economic conditions now well above subsistence levels in many Asian countries, consumer demand in the region is booming. Demand is fueled in part by the global information explosion, which heightens the awareness and expectations of hundreds of millions of people. It is also fueled by aging populations, a growing middle class, and rapid urbanization.

## Opportunities for American Businesses

The dynamic growth and richness of Asian markets present tremendous opportunities for American businesses. That's the good news. Unfortunately, there also is bad news; i.e., not only is the competition fierce in these markets, many Americans have failed to achieve success here. The reasons are many, but they center on a lack of flexibility, tenacity, or cultural understanding.

Yet many American firms succeed in Asia. Stories of several of them appear in this guide. And success does not depend on having the bankroll and resources of a large company. Quite to the contrary, the entrepreneurial spirit and personal commitment of smaller companies, and their willingness to enter into joint ventures and strategic alliances, often give these companies a comparative advantage over larger organizations.

What Americans need to penetrate Asian markets, in addition to their traditional can-do attitude, is a simple set of keys ... keys to success in Asia.

# Chapter 2

# The Keys to Success

---

**THINK GLOBAL, ACT LOCAL**

The phrase "Think Global, Act Local" is often used today to indicate the principal key to international business success. It means this: Conceive your business strategies with an eye to the global marketplace, but in any given place carry on your business and market your products and services with an eye to local customs and preferences.

The world is increasingly interdependent. There is hardly a place on earth that is not affected by a major economic change in one or more of the large industrial countries. If the United States sneezes, the rest of the world catches cold. If, on the other hand, an economic boom is underway in the United States, or Japan, or Germany, much of the rest of the world will find itself in good or improving health.

Global changes of all kinds have an impact on business. Political changes in Eastern Europe and the former Soviet Union are creating new opportunities and new competition. Shifts in military power are causing revisions to government spending and social agendas.

Accordingly, an American manufacturer of pollution control equipment needs to "think global"; needs to consider, for example, whether political, social, and economic conditions in Southeast Asia will create strong demand for the equipment there (and in which countries) and whether the American products will be able to compete successfully with equipment produced in Europe or Japan.

Finally, to make sales and achieve success, a company must "act local." It must design and market its products and services in ways that appeal to specific customers in the country in which the products will be sold. Business strategies and tactics that are effective in South Korea may be counter-productive if used in Indonesia.

**KNOW THE CUSTOMER**

To sell products and services in Asia, one must know the customer and the environment in which that customer makes decisions. This can be a daunting challenge for Americans doing business in Asia for the first time. Everything is "foreign"; the languages, the customs, the value systems, the business practices. Because detailed knowledge of—and sensitivity to—these broad and specific market conditions is one of the keys to business success in Asia, every American company *must* learn the ropes at the onset.

To achieve success in Asia, you need to study each separate country in which you plan to sell. Often you need to study separate market segments within a single country. Products popular in Taiwan might not be popular in Malaysia. Products that sell in urban Indonesia might not sell at all 100 miles west of Jakarta.

## ADAPT TO THE MARKET

Although Kentucky Fried Chicken is a big success in Japan today, it started out over twenty years ago in Tokyo in a very small way. Loy Weston, who went to Japan to start Kentucky Fried's operations there, credits much of KFC's success to the fact that they adapted the product to satisfy the needs of the market. By trial and error, he found that mashed potatoes did not sell in Japan but French fries did. He learned the coleslaw recipe was too sweet for the Japanese palate, so he reduced the sugar content.

In these and countless other ways Weston and his colleagues adjusted the product and their sales efforts to the preferences of the customer. They maintained the basic Kentucky Fried Chicken concepts, but — without compromising product quality — adapted those basic concepts and the product mix to satisfy local market requirements.

Not all products and services lend themselves to easy, country-by-country adaptation to Asian tastes ... but many do. More often than not, the marketing effort fails because there simply has been no effort made to adapt. Broadly stated, market failure for American companies in Asia frequently is the result of a lack of cultural understanding and equally inadequate market knowledge. Typically these companies assume that what appeals to American markets will appeal anywhere in the world. Nothing could be further from the truth.

## COMMITMENT, PATIENCE, PERSISTENCE

Asian cultures practice a higher degree of commitment, patience, and persistence in their business practices than do most Western cultures. Nowhere is this more true than in comparison of Asian philosophy and practice with American business culture, where a general lack of patience and an unwillingness to make long-term investments to reach long-term objectives typify a majority of American companies. This culture/business philosophy gap presents a double challenge to Americans who want to do business in Asia. Not only must they compete in unfamiliar markets, they must do so in a different and more demanding environment.

Many of the American companies that have succeeded in Asia have done so only after establishing a long-term presence there, demonstrating to potential customers a substantial commitment (not merely through local representatives), and being willing to endure years of losses before turning a profit. They stubbornly persisted in their efforts, trying again and again to make sales. They changed their approach or altered their product, "fine-tuning" their product/service offer, and often negotiating for days on end until they finally achieved success—sometimes on "one last try."

Why should American companies take the risks associated with doing business in Asia? Clearly some should not. Companies with products and services that would have no appeal in Asia should stay home. But companies that see opportunity for themselves in a global marketplace, whose existing markets may be vulnerable to foreign competition, must consider seriously the steps they must take to compete successfully in Asian markets.

## NETWORKING AND PARTNERING

The best way to enter an Asian market is to use your own networks to identify appropriate partners or representatives there. The decisions you make in doing so are perhaps the most critical of all, so you should not hurry the process. Talk to your business colleagues who have done business in the market you want to enter. Ask them to refer you to others who have done business there and talk to those people as well. Then go to the Asian country and meet a number of potential partners and representatives. Do not select any on that first trip. Do further investigation and return to the country again for additional talks and perhaps to meet others.

While you want to start doing business as quickly as possible, this is the time for careful, deliberate analysis, for checking every question, every reference. You will learn that some of the potential partners or representatives you interview are not everything they appear to be. More of this in Chapter 6.

Care in selecting partners and representatives is not only critical because of the key role these people will play in your ultimate success or failure, it also is important because, at this stage of your effort, you will lack essential knowledge of the Asian country and its business practices.

Entering an Asian market through a partnership or joint venture with a local business has many advantages over going in alone or only using representatives. A local partner will have a stake in the success of the venture. He will have indispensable connections. He also may have business strengths or product lines that complement your own.

## ADDITIONAL STRATEGIES

American exporters often find that Asian trading companies, especially those located in Japan, Hong Kong, and Singapore, are effective in marketing products in their own countries and elsewhere in Asia on behalf of American clients. These trading companies evaluate the potential of a product or service and work with the owner to adapt it to individual Asian markets, if necessary. They develop marketing and distribution plans and then handle the details. All of this is done for a fee, of course. Many of these trading companies, such as Sumitomo of Japan and Jardine Matheson of Hong Kong, have offices in various United States cities.

Another way for American exporters to participate in Asian markets is to become suppliers of American companies that already operate there, such as Hewlett-Packard, Procter & Gamble, and Eli Lilly and Company. In time, with knowledge gained as a supplier to such companies and with relationships developed with others operating in Asia, an exporter will be positioned to establish its own presence in Asian markets.

## GETTING HELP

Help is available not only from your own network of friends and business colleagues but also from many American business people who have hands-on experience in Asia. Your networks will lead you to some of these. Many will be happy to share their experiences with you. Others, who work as consultants, will serve you well for a fee. Again, a time to move with "deliberate speed," particularly in taking the time to check the qualifications and references of those who propose to work for you for a fee.

In addition, a wealth of information and assistance on doing business in Asia is available to American businesses from the U.S. Small Business Administration, the U.S. Department of Commerce, various chambers of commerce and business organizations, and the international trade offices of a number of U.S. states and Asian countries. The U.S. Department of Commerce in Singapore, for example, will arrange "Breakfast Briefings" enabling visiting Americans to meet a number of local business people, will display a company's materials in its library, and, for a reasonable fee, will provide basic consulting services. Resource organizations that provide such services are listed in Appendix A and in the country sections of Chapter 9.

## TRADE SHOWS

Attending or exhibiting at a trade show in Asia can be a useful way to "test the waters" for your products and services. It also is a good way to make connections and develop your knowledge and understanding of Asian markets.

There are dozens of trade shows held throughout Asia in the course of a year. Appendix B sets forth a number of the recent or planned Asian trade shows of interest to American exporters. These shows feature scores of exhibitors and attract thousands of visitors. Some are especially large, such as Singapore Informatics '93 (computers and peripherals) with over 1,200 exhibitors and more than 100,000 visitors. FoodEx Japan (food and beverage), with over 1,000 exhibitors, attracts more than 85,000 visitors.

To obtain information about Asian trade shows, American exporters should contact one or more of the resources listed in the country sections and Appendix A.

## ABOVE ALL, LEARN THE CULTURE

The master key to business success in Asia is cultural understanding.

Cultural understanding is more than just knowing the history and statistics that make up a country profile. It is the understanding one gains from the study of people and what makes them tick. It is the perception gained from listening, observing, and imagining yourself in the shoes of another. The best way to acquire cultural understanding is to spend time in the country in question. You need to go there.

To be successful in Japan, for example, you need to spend some time contemplating things that are uniquely Japanese; the elegant simplicity of *ikebana* floral arrangements, for example, or the boxes of perfectly matched fresh fruit displayed in shops along the side streets of Tokyo— even the pint-sized garbage trucks that navigate those streets. You will soon develop a feel for the qualities of style, precision, and scale that are so important to the Japanese; qualities that deeply affect their buying decisions.

You should not patronize an Asian culture, however, nor mimic it in your personal behavior. Asians expect Americans to be Americans. They do not expect Americans to bow precisely as they do when they greet each other or to handle chopsticks as well as silverware (but they do expect you to try the chopsticks, and developing some competence can be a plus). Rather, when Americans deal with them or sell them products or services, Asians expect Americans to be themselves, *and* to recognize and respect their individual cultures and practices.

A lot more needs to be said about the culture factor in Asia.

# Chapter 3

# The Culture Factor

It is a common human assumption that others throughout the world see, hear, smell, and feel things as we do. We assume that they experience the same physical, intellectual, and emotional reactions, with perhaps a few idiosyncratic exceptions. We believe that what is pleasing to us will be pleasing to others.

It also is a common assumption that people in one part of the world, like the people in Central America, or Southeast Asia, are all pretty much the same. This is not so. There are many differences within each region.

As global information systems expand our knowledge and understanding of the world's people, such mistaken assumptions are gradually disappearing. Nevertheless, such (often cliched) assumptions die hard. American business people who want to succeed overseas normally need to broaden considerably their understanding of the cultures and customs of their target markets.

Probably the most important key to success in Asia for an American is mastering the culture factor. Once this has been accomplished, the American will have a fair shot at evaluating Asian markets, designing and adapting products and services that will appeal to Asians, and working productively with Asian colleagues.

## INDIVIDUALISM AND COLLECTIVISM

There are two principal culture groupings in the world, individualist cultures and collectivist cultures. Asians are collectivists. Westerners are individualists. Comparing the two cultural groupings will help Americans understand Asians better.

Individualist cultures predominate in many of the Western countries: the United States, Australia, Canada, New Zealand, and parts of Western Europe. In these cultures, group goals are subordinated to personal goals; independence and personal achievement are valued highly, and discipline is often loose. The individual is the core of the social unit. People in these cultures cherish their freedoms, the right to free speech, the right to protest. They value candor and directness. They are accustomed to making independent decisions and taking independent action. They strive for personal accomplishment, eager to stand out from the crowd.

Collectivist cultures predominate in Asia, eastern Europe, Africa, and Latin America. Here personal goals are subordinated to group goals. The family and the employment organization are the core social units. Duty, harmony, politeness, and modesty are very important. Discipline is high. Individuals are not permitted to stand out from the crowd. As Confucius taught, "The nail that protrudes is hammered down."

Consistent with these characteristics, individualists tend to be the ones who excel in inventing things, and collectivists tend to be the ones who excel in activities that call for group effort, like manufacturing and servicing.

Perhaps it is the emphasis on harmony in collectivist cultures that makes Asians tend to be more intuitive and subtle in their thoughts and actions than Westerners, who tend to be more logical and linear in their responses and reasoning. Asians, for example, pay more attention to relationships than contracts, and Westerners pay more attention to deadlines and schedules than social protocol.

The most significant feature of collectivist cultures for American business people to understand is the emphasis on family and group ties. It is this feature that largely accounts for the close and often exclusive affiliations of local businesses in Asia. For example: the Japanese *keiretsu*, those groups of Japanese corporations like Mitsubishi or Sumitomo that are bound together by cross-stockholdings and tend to do business only with their corporate siblings, all else being equal. Or the Korean *chaebols*, the large conglomerates of that country. Or the vast networks of Chinese family-owned businesses in Taiwan, Hong Kong, and elsewhere in Asia.

This emphasis on family and group ties also accounts for the importance to Asians of long-term personal relationships. Whereas Americans are compulsive about getting down to business right away, sealing a deal with a written contract, and riding off in a cloud of dust to confront the next challenge, most Asians will want to develop a personal relationship with a business partner before making an agreement of any significance. Even then, it will take years before they will feel that a solid business relationship exists.

It is striking how dissimilar are the characteristics of the two cultural groupings in practice. Americans can easily appreciate collectivist values but they often have difficulty heeding them when they come into conflict with individualistic values. For example, an American might know that he is breaching the harmony of his relationship with an Asian by criticizing the Asian's performance in front of others, but the American will believe that it is more important to be open and forthright in his business dealings.

## CONFUCIANISM AND ISLAM

Philosophy and religion, particularly Confucianism and the Islamic religion, are other key ingredients of Asian cultures, and they tell much about the way business is done in Asia.

Confucius lived in the sixth century B.C. He founded a body of philosophy that spread throughout Asia and was incorporated in various ways in the fabric of life and in many of the religions of the area. This was especially true in East Asia. Confucianism holds, like collectivism generally, that the family unit is the root of social stability and political order and that an individual's identity is in terms of the family or group.

In addition, Confucianism teaches the improvability of the human condition; that hard work and self-cultivation in the context of group achievement is one's objective. In this connection, it teaches that education is the key to human development. It also teaches that the ultimate meaning of life is realized through ordinary, practical living.

There is much evidence of Confucian philosophy in Asian business practices. The training and education of employees, for example, is continual. Also, employers and employees tend to accept a strong commitment to each other, with many people working for only one employer for their entire careers.

Islam is the major religion in Indonesia and Malaysia, and it too teaches values that are relevant to commerce. Islam stresses the virtues of prosperity and hard work. It also emphasizes the importance of initiative and freedom of action.

These philosophical and religious underpinnings tend to support the group-oriented work ethic that prevails in much of Asia.

## HIERARCHY

Confucius taught that people are *un*equal rather than equal in terms of status. He also taught that a person's individual contributions in life must be in the context of the family or group. These views were held by other Asian philosophers and accepted by various religions in Asia. Consequently, in contrast to the individual attitudes prevalent in Western cultures, people in Asia are more willing to accept their fate and their status in society. They also are less inclined to seek personal recognition or reach for higher status.

These attitudes, coupled with emphasis on the recognition of elders and authority figures in a family or group, result in Asians giving greater weight to hierarchy in their business dealings than Westerners do. For example, Asians will want Americans to establish clearly the titles and positions they hold in their organizations. Asians need to understand these matters before any business can be done.

Accordingly, business cards are always exchanged in Asia because they serve to establish both individual and group identity and status. In many Asian countries it is helpful, and a sign of respect for your Asian colleagues, to have your cards printed in the appropriate Asian language on one side. Although you can do this on short notice in many Asian cities after your arrival, it is best to do it before departing on your trip to be certain that the translation is correct and the printing is well done. If you live in or near a large American city, there are printing and translating firms that can provide this service.

Also, letters of introduction from someone who knows both parties (such as a bank, consultant, or business associate) are important in Asia. Proper introductions are needed to establish identity and status. When Americans request appointments by writing or faxing an Asian who does not already know them, they often receive no response because the Asian considers them to be outsiders. This may strike Americans as unacceptably rude business behavior. To an Asian, however, no obligation is owed an outsider.

Finally, Americans will need to be sensitive to the relative status of people. If an American accidentally gives equal or greater deference to an Asian executive's underling, the executive will be offended. Also, Americans will find that Asians work within well-defined roles. If an American asks an Asian engineer to comment on a marketing plan, the engineer will probably not respond or will be uncomfortable in doing so.

## DECISION MAKING

In keeping with collectivism, decision making in Asian cultures is much more consultative than in Western cultures. Typically, any major decision in an Asian family or group is made only after wide review and discussion by all persons concerned.

This has major implications for Americans who do business with Asians. It means that meetings will take longer, and will be recessed more often, than Americans would think necessary. Asians in meetings will want to make certain they understand points of discussion well so that they can later review them with their colleagues outside the room. They will need recesses in order to confer with those colleagues. Asians often take copious notes in meetings for this reason. Sometimes meetings will break off for days on end while Asians consult and Americans cool their heels in their hotel rooms or even return home.

It may seem to Americans that discussions and negotiations take an inordinately long time. On the other hand, decisions arrived at Asian-style tend to be sound and easily executed. All implications and repercussions will have been carefully considered, and implementation issues will have been well thought out.

## EDUCATION

The role and style of education in Asia, especially in the countries where Confucian philosophies prevail, are important to note. Education is considered the key to human development in these countries. Combined with an ethic of hard work, many Asians spend extraordinary amounts of time and effort in schools. South Korea leads all others in this respect. Its children spend 240 days in school every year, attending six days a week and eight hours a day. Compare this to United States averages of 180 days per year and six hours a day.

Because of the cultural importance of hard work, duty, obedience, and group connections, the style of education in Asia is highly diligent but somewhat methodical. The assertions of professors and teachers are seldom questioned. Imaginative thinking is often discouraged. At college and graduate school levels, students who get into the better schools by dint of talent, hard work, or connections, often relax their efforts after admission.

Americans who do business in Asia need to recognize and understand the importance of education to Asians. They can expect Asians to be knowledgeable on many subjects, and eager to learn more, but sometimes resistant to new ideas.

## THE ROLE OF GOVERNMENT

In keeping with their collectivist cultures, the governments of Asian countries play a supportive and developmental role for their people, not just a regulatory or supervisory role. Accordingly, Asian governments are highly active in the economic and private sectors of their countries. In contrast to most Western governments, they are hands-on, not hands-off, in their dealings with business. Relations between government and business tend to be closer. It is this collaborative role that has led to Japan's dynamic growth—and to the label "Japan Inc."—and has contributed to the rapid economic growth of Singapore, to cite two examples.

Americans who are new to business in Asia are often surprised by the extent of government bureaucracy and red tape. After they have worked in Asia for a time, they are pleased to discover a positive, cooperative attitude on the part of most government officials. However, they tend to find their most effective strategy is to leave to their local partners and representatives the task of obtaining government clearances and approvals.

## THE CHINESE CONNECTION

It also is important to note the extensive networks of Chinese in Asia. Collectivist, linguistic, and ethnic connections of the Chinese provide the most far-reaching and cohesive linkages in the region. Moreover, the ethnic Chinese have proved themselves highly successful in commerce, not only in Taiwan, Singapore, and Hong Kong, but recently in China as well. Also, overseas Chinese control significant segments of business in Indonesia, Malaysia, and elsewhere in Asia where they are an ethnic minority. Singapore-based Chinese who operate in Indonesia, for example, are very astute in their selection of local partners.

Americans need to be aware of these linkages. It is useful but often difficult to tap into them. In addition, in countries like Indonesia and Malaysia, where the Chinese are resented in some quarters for their economic power and influence (note that this resentment can be ameliorated by the selection of national associates who are respected and politically-aware), Americans need to consider the political and social consequences of alliances with the Chinese.

## GIFT-GIVING AND ENTERTAINMENT

While Americans do not normally attach much significance to gift-giving and business entertainment in the context of their business relationships, these matters are especially important throughout Asia. Gift-giving and entertainment are things that sales people do for their major customers, usually once a year at Christmas or when a customer celebrates some milestone. Most American business people feel somewhat awkward in giving gifts and entertaining or reciprocating. Often they do not know what to do or when to do it, and they worry that the gesture might be inadequate or misinterpreted.

In Asia, however, where interpersonal relations are paramount in business, gift-giving and entertainment are as important as the drafting of a contract. They are accorded the utmost attention, and are practiced as an art form.

Americans need first to recognize that gift-giving and entertainment are an integral part of business in Asia. One story relates how a typical hard-charging American business executive, eager to consummate the deal that he had flown to Tokyo to arrange, was very pleased when his Japanese counterpart invited him to play a round of golf soon after he arrived. He enjoyed the game immensely and was invited to play again the next day. On the following day, his host suggested that they play again, and he asked, "But when are we going to start doing business?" His host, surprised, responded, "But we have been doing business."

Americans who do business in Asia need to devote careful attention to gift-giving and entertainment. A few general points are made below. Specific points are made in the country sections that follow.

Gifts should be pertinent to the nature of a relationship or transaction. Generally, appropriateness and thoughtfulness are much more important than value. Lavish gifts normally should be avoided because they place too great a burden of obligation on the recipient. The best gifts an American can give often are items that are distinctively American or can be identified with the giver's organization or region. Here are some examples:

- American Indian art or jewelry
- American magazine subscriptions
- Audio tapes of famous American orchestras or recording stars
- Books, especially albums with photographs of American scenes
- Calendars with American scenes
- Coffee mugs with logos
- Disney items
- Golf balls with a company logo
- Hawaiian macadamia nuts
- Name brand items from noted American stores, such as Saks Fifth Avenue, L. L. Bean, Tiffany, Bloomingdale's, Neiman Marcus
- Packets of postcards with American scenes
- Pens or desk sets with a company logo
- T-shirts with American sports or university emblems
- U.S. coin sets or postage stamp sets
- U.S. road atlases
- U.S. wines or whiskeys (except not for Muslims)
- Vermont maple syrup

Attention also should be given to a gift's wrapping and presentation. Wrapping customs, and the significance of the color of wrapping paper, will vary from country to country. The general rule is that wrapping should be neat and simple. Gifts should be presented and received with both hands and never in an offhand manner. In most Asian countries a gift is not opened in the presence of the giver because the gift might not be appropriate or might be too lavish and might embarrass the recipient or others present. Therefore, Americans should not insist that their presents to others be opened, and they should put aside the gifts they receive unless their Asian friends repeatedly insist that they open them immediately.

If you are taking gifts into Asia, do not wrap them ahead of time because customs officials will ask you to unwrap them. Rather, carry the wrapping paper separately or have your gifts wrapped locally in Asia.

The timing for giving a gift can be important. Often a small gift is given at the first of several anticipated meetings, with the implied hope "that this friendship will last." A larger gift is then given at the close of the final meeting.

If you are unsure about the protocol and timing of gift-giving, it is best to let your Asian hosts make the first move. However, be prepared to reciprocate before leaving town.

Similarly, as to entertainment, Americans visiting an Asian country should usually let their Asian hosts lead the way. Then, at an appropriate time before returning home, they should reciprocate in some comparable manner.

Dining with your Asian friends and colleagues affords an excellent opportunity to expand your cultural understanding and to strengthen your personal and business relationships with them. Consistent with the emphasis on personal relationships in Asian cultures, dining is more of a social and cultural event in Asia than it is a nourishment of the body. A meal should not be rushed, and careful attention should be given to ceremony and etiquette.

Asians do not expect Americans to be accomplished practitioners of Asian dining customs. You can ask for a knife and fork if you are not comfortable with using chopsticks when eating with Japanese, Koreans, and ethnic Chinese. However, your gestures of interest and respect in observing their customs and trying local foods will be greatly appreciated. Also, if you are the host, you may need to remember that Muslims do not eat pork (including ham and bacon) and Buddhists do not eat beef (including veal).

## GESTURES, BODY LANGUAGE, AND COLORS

Asians tend to be more sensitive to gestures, body language, and colors than Americans are. Each country has somewhat different cultural traditions and codes of conduct in these matters, but a few general observations can be made.

Gestures and behavior that disrupt harmony or indicate a lack of respect are normally unacceptable. For example, challenging gestures, such as placing your hands on your hips or waving a fist, are considered highly offensive. Other gestures, such as pointing or beckoning with a finger, are considered rude. (Asians often use the thumb, with fingers clenched below it, to point at something.) Whistling or snapping fingers to get the attention of a waiter is also rude, as is pointing a toe or exposing the sole of your shoe toward another person.

Casual body contact is also generally unacceptable in Asia. Americans, even in a flush of camaraderie, should resist an impulse to clap an Asian on the back or pat him on the shoulder. Touching a person on the head is especially offensive in Southeast Asia. Unless your Asian counterpart takes the lead in being more demonstrative physically, shaking hands is about as far as an American should go anywhere in Asia.

Traditions of harmony and respect also give rise to greater formality and polite behavior in meetings and at dinners than Americans normally observe. Visitors and important guests will usually be given a place of honor, often facing the entrance door in a meeting room or next to the host at a dinner. Americans should let their hosts indicate where they should sit. Posture in meetings can also be important, especially in Japan and Korea where slouching and other sloppy meeting habits are offensive.

Colors often have important associations and meanings for Asians. Black is avoided in most Asian countries because of its association with death. In Japan, white also is avoided for this reason. Red and gold are good luck colors in Chinese cultures. However, the Chinese associate red ink with the severance of relationships, and the Japanese use red ink for death notices. Some colors, like yellow in Malaysia, are avoided in personal wear because they are the colors of royalty. Accordingly, Americans should consult their Asian friends and colleagues as to the significance of colors in the clothing they intend to wear on important occasions, in gift wrapping, and in their marketing and presentation materials.

## THE NEXT STEP

Armed with a set of the keys to success, including the key of cultural insight, an American is ready to seek out Asian business opportunities.

# Chapter 4

# Where the Opportunities Are

Until quite recently, when most American business people thought about their sales opportunities, they limited their aspirations to the United States. And why not? The United States was and will continue to be a rich and diverse market.

Today, Americans see a global marketplace and face stiff competition at home and abroad. Some of their toughest competitors come from abroad. Of necessity, American businesses today, like their competition, must seek out distant markets to develop and sustain growth.

Opportunities today are global. For Americans, some of the greatest opportunities that lie ahead are in Asia. In order to sort out where the opportunities will be for Americans in Asia, one needs to understand the factors that influence Asian markets and drive the economic growth of the region.

This chapter discusses those factors.

## ATTITUDES TOWARD AMERICAN PRODUCTS AND SERVICES

To begin on an optimistic note, let us recognize that there generally is a high regard throughout Asia for things American. Sure, the United States has plenty of detractors in Asia, mostly critics of U.S. policy and influence. And there are many in Asia who feel that the workmanship and design of some American products are inadequate, or that the quality— even the relevance—of some services are off the mark. But largely there is a substantial liking and respect in Asia for American style, innovation, and technology.

Americans need not hang their heads in Asia, at least so long as they demonstrate a reciprocal respect and understanding for their Asian customers, colleagues and competitors ... and offer products that meet accepted quality standards.

## THE INFORMATION EXPLOSION

Americans have a high profile in Asia, as they do elsewhere in the world, in part because of the global information explosion that occurred in recent years. Thanks to CNN and other enterprising international media, images and events from throughout the world now reach the most remote villages and kampongs of Asia in matters of minutes. American accomplishments and lifestyles (and misadventures) seldom are overlooked in the process.

Satellite transmission of news and entertainment now reaches vast numbers of people. In 1991, AsiaSat I began broadcasting from Hong

Kong. AsiaSat I has a footprint that covers 38 countries, from Japan to Egypt, Mongolia to Indonesia, reaching 2.7 billion people, well over half the people in the world. This coverage is extended by Indonesia's Palapa satellite. Two additional satellites, AsiaSat II and Orbx-2, will be in the skies by the mid-1990s, making satellite TV virtually global.

The BBC now beams news, sports and entertainment from AsiaSat, and it broadcasts in Mandarin as well as English. It will soon also broadcast in Hindi. Other language channels will follow. Now MTV also broadcasts from AsiaSat. More and more households and communities can afford the TV sets and satellite dishes needed to receive these broadcasts. Some governments, such as Malaysia and Singapore, that are traditionally sensitive to public opinion prohibit the unlicensed use of satellite dishes but are having mixed results in enforcing their controls.

The significance of these developments is that the awareness and expectations of hundreds of millions of people are rising dramatically, fueling consumer demand to the extent that incomes permit.

## POPULATION CHANGES

Changes in the composition, movements, and habits of populations in Asia are having an enormous impact on business opportunities there. People are living longer. Population growth rates are declining. There are more households, more people are moving to the cities. Perhaps most important, in terms of increasing market potential, there is a growing middle class.

Life expectancy in Indonesia, for example, is expected to rise from its 1960-65 rate of 42.5 years to 63.4 years by 2005. Population growth rates in Malaysia and Singapore, 2.6 percent and 1.2 percent respectively in the 1980s, are expected to fall by about half, to 1.4 percent and 0.6 percent, by 2010. There will be proportionally fewer children, but more young adults, middle-aged, and elderly. For example, children between the ages of 5 and 14 in 1980 made up 26.4 percent of Thailand's population. By 2010, this segment will have decreased to 16 percent. Conversely, older people will make up a larger share of the population. In Indonesia, those aged 65 and over in 1980 were only 3.3 percent of the population. By 2010 they will comprise 6.3 percent.

As the economies of Asian countries develop and urban infrastructure and employment grow, populations are shifting from rural settings to the cities, from agricultural activities to industrial and services employment. The population of Jakarta, Indonesia, for example, is expected to grow within the next ten years from its present 9.4 million people to 13.2 million people.

All of this indicates growing consumer demand in Asia. Older populations will be able to travel more and buy more, and they will need more medical products and care. Urbanization will mean home construction and demand for appliances, furnishings, electronics, and financial services. And with higher standards of living, there will be greater demand for luxury goods and entertainment.

## STAGES OF DEVELOPMENT, STANDARDS OF LIVING

Opportunities for American exporters in any given Asian country have a great deal to do with that country's stage of economic development. The nature and amount of the goods and services the population will demand depend on the sophistication of its economy, the extent to which its government plays a role in stimulating growth, and the amount of money people have to spend.

The industrialized countries of Asia, like Japan, South Korea, and Taiwan, now demand highly sophisticated goods and services: for example, advanced manufacturing technology, upscale consumer items, and complex financial services. Such developing Asian countries as Indonesia and Thailand need more basic things, like electronic equipment, industrial chemicals, and engineering services.

On average, people in the advanced countries have a lot of money to spend. In Japan, the gross domestic product per capita is about $27,200. The higher the standard of living, of course, the more opportunities there are to sell such luxury items and services as expensive apparel, travel, and entertainment.

People in the large developing countries have much less to spend. In China, the gross domestic product per capita is about $360; in Indonesia, about $630. However, the governments of some of Asian countries, like Taiwan, Malaysia and Indonesia, are spending heavily on expanded infrastructure and other development schemes.

The status of infrastructure development is an opportunity factor in itself. Inadequate infrastructure inhibits growth; extensive infrastructure encourages growth. For expanding opportunities, American exporters of consumer goods should look for Asian markets that are supported by ample seaports, transportation systems, electrical generating capabilities, and urban facilities. On the other hand, Americans who market products and services needed for infrastructure build-up should look for opportunities in those countries that are investing heavily in their infrastructure.

## THE EXPANDING ROLE OF WOMEN

Women are entering the work forces of Asia at a rapid rate, in part because they are demanding an enlarged role in their societies and in part because personnel shortages are appearing at all levels of both the public and private sectors. This is especially true in Singapore, Taiwan, and Hong Kong. There is resistance to this movement in Japan and South Korea, countries that are particularly male-oriented. However, the need to admit more women into the ranks of workers and management there is compelling, and attitudes are beginning to change.

The presence of more women in the work force means that more products and services will be bought by women. To an increasing extent, marketing efforts will need to appeal to women's needs and perspectives. Products and services for working women, such as upscale women's clothing and convenience foods, will be in greater demand.

## TOURISM

By the year 2000, tourism in Asia is expected to double from its present levels. This will be due in part to the growing wealth of the region, enabling more Asians to travel. It will also be the result of the growing attractiveness of Asia as a tourist destination for people from other parts of the world.

Tourism growth suggests many opportunities for American firms: transportation, consulting services, entertainment, hotel equipment and supplies, publishing, resort apparel, luxury goods.

## GOVERNMENT POLICIES

Trade and development policies should not be overlooked as factors influencing opportunities in an Asian country.

All of the countries discussed in this guide impose import tariffs on various products that compete with their own products. All of them, however, are proponents of free trade and are working toward the reduction of trade barriers. An American firm needs to investigate carefully what tariffs and other barriers apply to its products and services in any given country.

On the positive side, national priorities are an important source of emerging opportunities, affecting public and private markets alike. National security issues continue to fuel the purchase of military equipment and supplies by Asian governments. In addition, many Asian countries recently commenced ambitious environmental programs, creating strong markets for American suppliers of pollution control equipment, technology, and services.

Other policies also affect opportunities in different ways, some of them negative. Governments sensitive to religious factions, such as Malaysia and Indonesia, periodically discourage excessive behavior, thus affecting markets for luxury goods. China cracks down on various indulgent business activities from time to time. In addition, governmental trade negotiations occasionally result in the shrinkage or expansion of markets for certain goods and services. Japan, for example, recently agreed to purchase greater numbers of automobile parts from the United States and to increase imports of various other products. Although actions like these are difficult to anticipate, American firms need to be alert to government policy changes in Asia and to remember that government and industry tend to be partners working toward mutually-agreed objectives.

## SEIZING THE OPPORTUNITIES

Woody Allen once quipped that eighty percent of being successful is showing up. He meant that people who embark on a project (his specific reference was to screen writers) have to follow through if they are to succeed.

Americans who identify opportunities in Asia will next need to seize those opportunities in business negotiations with their Asian counterparts.

# Chapter 5

# Business Negotiations

In business dealings with Asians, Americans need to keep in mind the collectivist cultural characteristics outlined in Chapter 3. In particular, Americans need to understand and appreciate Asian businessmen desire to maintain harmony with their business associates, to establish long-term relationships, and to consider matters in a careful and thorough manner.

## LOOK FOR DIFFERENCES IN STYLE AND APPROACH

Americans will also find it helpful to contrast their own negotiating styles with those of Asians. Americans normally want to "win" each negotiation. They strive to get the better of the other side, ignoring possible repercussions that may affect future deals. At the end of the negotiation they work toward a "meeting of minds" and a signed contract that, to them, represents the ultimate success.

Most Asians, however, seeking harmony, hope that a negotiation will lead to a mutually beneficial arrangement and a long relationship with many additional deals to follow. They look for a "meeting of hearts." A signed contract is only a beginning. It's the relationship that counts. Whereas an American will try to resolve all potentially conflicting issues during the negotiations and in the written contract, an Asian will try to establish a relationship that will enable the parties to resolve conflicts in the future.

Americans treat a negotiation as a step-by-step problem-solving exercise. They try to get agreement on points as the negotiation proceeds, saving the big points for last but not later giving any thought to renegotiating the earlier ones. For Asians, however, nothing is settled until the very last. Even then, after a contract is signed, Asians feel it's entirely proper to renegotiate a provision that has an unfair result.

The head negotiator for an American organization usually has broad decision-making authority. He has been empowered to commit the organization on the spot. Typically, this person is accompanied by only a small team of assistants. Asian negotiators, on the other hand, won't make any major decisions until there have been exhaustive consultations with their colleagues inside and outside the negotiating room. They often have a large negotiating team, and the person who speaks for the group is not necessarily its leader. Sometimes this person is designated the spokesman because of his superior language skills.

Asian negotiators tend to adopt firm bargaining positions and give ground reluctantly. This is partly because their positions have been refined beforehand through elaborate consultations within their organization.

Americans tend to be less rigidly committed and to have a number of fall-back positions. To Americans, many Asians seem stubborn and unwilling to compromise. To Asians, many Americans—because of their negotiating flexibility—seem inconsistent and insincere.

While Asians tend to be inflexible during negotiations and flexible as to the terms of the deal after a contract is signed, Americans tend to be just the opposite.

## ETIQUETTE COUNTS

Cultural etiquette can cause misunderstandings. Whereas Americans have no difficulty in saying "no," Asian negotiators, reluctant to give offense, shy away from confrontations and find it difficult to give a negative response. They will say, "It is very difficult . . .." or "We need to think about this . . ." or "Let us get back to you on that." A long delay in giving a response is often the Asians' polite way of saying no, although it could merely be due to a perceived need for lengthy consultations within their organization or a means of indicating that an important point is being given careful consideration.

A "yes" by an Asian in a meeting could mean at least one of three things. It could mean, "I understand what you said but I don't necessarily agree." It could mean, "I don't understand what you said but I don't want to offend you, or embarrass myself, by saying I don't understand you." It could also mean, "I agree." In a negotiation, however, it probably does not mean the latter.

Similarly, an Asian's laughter in meetings may not indicate amusement. Often it is an embarrassed response when the Asian does not understand the American's point or simply does not wish to reply.

It is well for Americans to remember that many Asians are masters of subtlety and indirection, talents owed to their traditions of maintaining harmony. For example, in a case where an Asian's sanity is being threatened by a neighbor's child who practices the piano until midnight day after day, she might say to the child's mother, "Your child is so accomplished. She practices so hard, until very late at night." That remark to an Asian is just as effective as the direct approach of an American who might say, "Your child kept me up until midnight with her piano practicing. How about shutting her down at nine p.m. in the future?"

## TIME GOES BY

A final contrast in American and Asian negotiating practices has to do with time. Although most Asians are highly punctual, and consider it discourteous not to be, they have not yet come to believe, as Americans do, that time is money. A negotiation will last for as long as it takes. Important matters cannot be rushed. After all, it is a long-term relationship that is being forged.

Americans, on the other hand, have little micro chips implanted in their brains that constantly remind them of the dollar value of the passing minutes, of opportunities lost, of flights missed, and of damage done to their careers by the slippage of schedules.

When there is a lull in discussions at a negotiation, Americans feel compelled to fill the void with talk, often pointless talk. Or they will needlessly make some concession in order to move things along. Americans also feel compelled to set deadlines, which normally works to their disadvantage. As a deadline approaches, they will concede points just to stick to a schedule that they themselves have set. Asian businessmen tend not to impose such artificial constraints on their negotiating and decision-making.

**SIX TIPS**

Here are six basic tips for conducting business negotiations in Asia.

**START SOCIALLY.** Host a cocktail reception, luncheon, or dinner for the negotiating teams. The other side probably will do the same. Don't plan to launch into meetings for a couple of days. And don't talk business at these social events. Get to know the other negotiators. Ask about their families, their organization, their group interests. These are the things that are most important to them. Hobbies and sports are good topics, too, but if you talk politics, be careful not to criticize or speak of conflicts. Asians can be very patriotic and nationalistic.

Use these social occasions to assess relationships on the other team. Unlike most Americans, Asians—especially the Japanese—are highly status conscious. It is prudent not to slight an Asian by giving one of his underlings greater deference or more attention. Asians are careful about such things. Sometimes, however, when the American team leader is a woman, they fail to accord her appropriate recognition. This is especially true in Japan and Korea, countries where it is unusual for a woman to hold a leading management position.

**BEGIN WITH A WELL-PREPARED OVERVIEW.** Without boasting, emphasize all the positive things that you can think of concerning your organization, the proposed project, and the future relationship of the parties. Stress the mutual benefits that can accrue from the deal. Avoid detail at this stage and try to present the proposed deal in broad outline. Asians like to see the forest first and then the trees. Speak deliberately. Take lots of time. Don't rush it or create any sense of pressure. Use visual aids and provide written materials. Complimentary reviews of your past work and news stories about your organization are especially effective since they provide assessments by third parties. Again, Asians are status- and group-conscious. They want to be associated with winners as much as they want to make a profit.

**BE PATIENT.** Once negotiations are underway, be prepared to give lengthy explanations and review issues over and over. Be prepared also for long recesses and delays while the Asian side adjourns to consult within its organization or reconsider its position on a point. Americans will be the more severely tested here, but Asians, in turn, will have to understand and be patient with American impatience. Asians become very involved in detail and want to assess all of the peripheral issues, issues that Americans are willing to gloss over or leave to be worked out after a contract is signed.

As a rule, it is best not to disclose your departure plans or impose any deadlines. Not only will this further bind you to your schedule, it will give the other side a negotiating lever as pressures build to conclude discussions.

Be comforted with the thought that long hours of negotiation can serve three very useful purposes. First, the parties will build a relationship that will become even more important than the resulting written contract. Second, many potential misunderstandings arising from cultural differences and communications barriers will be avoided. Third, discussions of peripheral issues will iron out implementation problems that might arise after a contract is signed, thus saving a lot of time and grief down the line.

**MAINTAIN HARMONY.** Think of positive ways to present an issue. Try not to be confrontational, and don't press too hard. Don't flatly reject anything. Americans tend to be direct and aggressive in their business dealings, but Asians also need to exercise self control. Some Asians, especially the Koreans, often become emotional and aggressive during negotiations. A frequent Asian response when nerves are frayed is to "shame" the other side for one failing or another.

A good way to promote harmony is to practice very good manners. Americans should avoid their customary informality. Use last names only. With Chinese in the People's Republic of China, use titles. Scrupulously observe rankings in seating arrangements and introductions. Do not interrupt; this is considered very rude. Don't openly disagree with your own teammates. Don't talk loudly or act in any way that indicates you believe you are superior. Don't show impatience through facial expressions or "body English." If you make a remark that appears to give offense, don't hesitate to apologize.

**NEVER UNDERESTIMATE THE LANGUAGE BARRIER.** Most Asians who are involved in international business are comfortable in negotiating in English, but it is still a second language for them. Americans should not abuse their good fortune by being careless with language. You should not talk too quickly or use slang or jargon. Don't move on to a new point until the point you have just made seems fully understood. Bear in mind that words will probably be taken literally. If you say to Asians that you believe your interests are "parallel" to theirs, they might wonder why your interests do not "converge" with theirs or are not the "same."

An American politician once visited China and spoke to a group of Chinese with the help of an interpreter. With typical American forthrightness, he said, "I'm going to tell you where I'm coming from." The interpreter said, "He'll now give you the name of his home town." Then he said, "I'm going to lay all my cards on the table." The interpreter said, "He'll play cards now." Then, resurrecting an old Will Rogers line, he said, "I'm not a member of any organized political party; I'm a Democrat." The interpreter said, "I think our guest just made a joke. Please laugh." The audience laughed and the politician knew he had their rapt attention.

The point here is that jokes as well as slang expressions should be avoided.

Incidentally, it is useful to have an interpreter on your side in cross-cultural negotiations, even if the negotiations are in your own language. An interpreter can help clarify points, counsel you on the best way to present certain issues, and advise you on the reactions of the other side. However, whenever there are interpreters involved in your discussions, be certain that they have an adequate command of the technical language used.

**KEEP THE DOCUMENTATION SIMPLE BUT CLEAR.** While Asians will consider the resulting relationship more binding than a written contract, you will be well served by ending up with a carefully documented agreement. The contract itself need not be as complex as a typical American contract. Schedules of procedures and technical data can be appended to the contract rather than incorporated into it. And lengthy clauses dealing with breach and default and other negative issues should be avoided.

Normally, a clause that requires the parties to resolve disputes harmoniously by conciliation is more effective.

This brings up a final issue, that of involving lawyers in negotiations. Most Asians view the presence of lawyers at business meetings as a sign of distrust. Accordingly, it's best to consult with your lawyer outside the meetings, or bring in the lawyer during the final phase to help with documentation.

## OTHER TIPS

Time-conscious Americans who do business in Asia often want to start work soon after they arrive. If you are one of these, you should plan instead to rest for a couple of days after arrival before doing any serious business. Jet lag adversely affects your patience and judgment. This is especially important if there will be negotiations, since the Asians will expect to put in long hours. If you are to achieve your desired results, you will need to be well rested.

Also, be clear about your position in your organization and your authority for concluding the business at hand. Hierarchy is important to Asians, and you will not make much progress until they know where you stand. Remember that titles can be confusing. Asians know that there can be owners with small interests, partners with little influence, presidents and CEOs of subsidiaries with limited authority, and vice presidents of all colors and flavors. Take time at the outset of your meetings to describe your position and authority and that of each of your associates. Don't exaggerate. Clarity and honesty here are essential.

For similar reasons, you will not make much progress if you send a junior executive to do the negotiating. The Asians will question your sincerity, your respect for them, and your interest in the proposed transaction. They will also assign their own lower-level executives to the discussions. Everything will move more slowly if it moves at all.

Finally, do not expect quick decisions. As collectivists, Asians make decisions on the basis of consensus. Many decisions during the course of negotiations will be made by the Asian side only after lengthy consultations with their colleagues outside the meeting room. A recess can go on for days. For these occasions, Americans should pack several good books and some audio tapes.

## A MULTIPLE OF TWO

The length and complexity of business negotiations depend on the nature of the deal. The bigger the deal, the longer and more detailed the negotiation. In negotiations with Asians, Americans should simply apply a multiplier of two to each of three basic elements of a negotiation: Double the amount of preparation; double the estimated time the negotiations will take; double the intensity of the effort.

If negotiations involve establishment of a joint venture or strategic alliance, where future relationships will be a major factor in success or failure, Americans should apply a multiplier of three.

# Chapter 6

# Joint Ventures & Strategic Alliances

Entering an Asian market through a partnership or joint venture with a local business has many advantages over going in alone or only using representatives. A local partner will know how to get things done. It will have a stake in the long-term success of the enterprise, not merely an interest in earning commissions and fees. Ideally, it will have something of real value to contribute to your efforts, such as well-developed markets for compatible products or services.

## WHEN ONE PLUS ONE EQUALS MORE THAN TWO

The terms partnership, joint venture, and strategic alliance are essentially synonymous. Each is a business arrangement among two or more participants to pursue a single enterprise. The idea is that the participants together can accomplish more together than any one can alone. For these arrangements to succeed, each participant needs to make a substantive contribution. The term "strategic alliance" has become fashionable in recent years to describe an arrangement that furthers the independent strategic goals of the participants. An example of an American-Asian strategic alliance might be one in which an Asian distributor of pollution control devices wants to expand its product lines with equipment manufactured by an American firm and the American firm wants to extend its markets to Asia.

Asians are especially interested in joint ventures and strategic alliances that give them access to American technology and know-how, including management know-how. While Americans need to be careful not to give away their technology and know-how, there are many ways to obtain fair compensation for them and to leverage their value in joint ventures and strategic alliances with Asian partners.

For American exporters of products and services, an Asian partner can often provide market access through its existing distribution and marketing networks. For American firms that need to establish manufacturing capabilities or representation offices in an Asian country, a local partner can often supply facilities and personnel. Also, an enterprise with a local partner can often gain access to import financing and circumvent trade barriers otherwise applicable to American firms who try to operate independently.

## BUILDING FOR THE FUTURE

Perhaps the most important benefit American firms derive from joint ventures and strategic alliances is the knowledge they gain about doing business in Asia and in building long-term relationships there. For these benefits to be realized, it is essential that American firms not leave the business in the hands of the Asian partner. Rather, they should take every opportunity to expand their participation and extend their relationships.

Americans should not view Asian partners as stepping stones, however. They should view them as foundations for expanding networks. Accordingly, Americans should select as partners those Asian firms that provide the best potential for solid, long-term relationships.

## SELECT WITH CARE

The risk inherent in any business relationship, of course, is that the participants will not get along and the enterprise will fail for lack of collaborative effort. The risk rises when the parties have incompatible objectives or do not understand each other well. Also, the higher the stakes, the more potentially fragile the bond. In cross-cultural enterprises, these factors are especially sensitive.

Accordingly, American firms that establish joint ventures and strategic alliances in Asia need to select their partners with great care. To identify potential partners, they should talk with their own networks and with other American firms that do business in Asia. They might also work with consultants and accounting firms that do business in Asia. Often such firms have excellent connections with Asian business people and specialize in organizing new ventures.

When several potential partners have been identified, the American firm can then commence a get-acquainted process with meetings and talks, at first on a very social level. The process should not be rushed. (As lawyers are fond of saying, move with all *deliberate* speed.) A selection should be made only after there is a very comfortable feeling about the partner selected and confidence that the selection process has been thorough.

Even large corporations need to select their partners with care. McDonald's Corporation recently opened its first outlet in China, capping an effort that commenced five years earlier. It is the largest McDonald's yet, situated in a new two-story structure near Tiananmen Square in the heart of Beijing. Well knowing the importance of partnerships and with much experience in other Asian countries, McDonald's spent three full years in its efforts to identify an appropriate Chinese business partner. The company's senior executive for the Asia-Pacific region, Noel Kaplan, met personally in Beijing with eight separate groups contending for the chance to be McDonald's partner in China. Mr. Kaplan made more than a dozen trips to China in the course of selecting the right partner.

Ultimately, the selection was not the group that promised the most or appeared at first to have the best connections or the greatest amount of applicable business experience. Rather, it was a group that had sound qualifications in all respects and, more importantly, struck all of the right chords of compatibility and philosophy during long discussions with Mr. Kaplan and his team.

## THE INDIRECT APPROACH

The best joint venture or strategic alliance for an American firm is not necessarily with a local Asian partner. It could be with another American firm already established in Asia or with an Asian firm of one country that has operations in another. You might well have a product or service, or some special technology or expertise, that such a firm needs to expand its existing business in Asia.

Taking this indirect approach in partnership with an Asian firm has great potential. For example, an alliance with a Hong Kong firm could be an excellent vehicle for opening up markets in China. An alliance with a Japanese firm in one or more of its ventures in Southeast Asia could be advantageous for both parties. Southeast Asia is an area where Americans and American products are well liked but where the Japanese, because of their military occupancy during World War II, often are not.

## THE FRINGE BENEFIT

Americans who enter into joint ventures and strategic alliances with Asians often develop closer ties with their Asian colleagues than Americans who do business in Asia through branch offices, agents, and representatives. In joint ventures and strategic alliances, Asians are more prepared to accept their American partners as members of their own inner circles. The result is that Americans who have Asian partners are exposed to a greater array of opportunities. They also gain greater insight into Asian culture and business practices. This is especially valuable in matters involving marketing, advertising, and distribution in Asia.

## Chapter 7

# Marketing, Advertising & Distribution

Sam Goldwyn, the movie producer known for his humorous misuse of the English language, once said, "When people aren't buying, there's no stopping them."

As sales executives know, there is more to business success than coming up with an excellent product or service. Potential customers must be made aware of it, be convinced that they need or want it, and be able to get their hands on it. Advertising, sales promotion, and distribution of products and services in the United States are substantial industries in themselves, employing millions of people. Large manufacturing and service companies have sizable departments devoted to these activities. When it comes to selling—all elements of marketing, in fact—Americans have the know-how.

Americans also lead the world in developing marketing techniques that become commonplace in the United States and elsewhere. For example, Americans were the first to demonstrate the value of market research and the appeal of supermarkets and discount stores. They struggle, however, when they encounter cultural differences and inefficient distribution systems. As Sam Goldwyn might say, "When Americans aren't selling in Asia, there's no stopping them."

**AMERICANS' CULTURAL BLINDERS**

In international marketing, American firms frequently make the mistake of assuming that what appeals in the United States will appeal elsewhere. To the contrary, cultural differences deeply affect the way people perceive things. This applies not only to a particular product or service, but applies also to the manner in which a product or service is advertised, packaged, and promoted.

Often advertising campaigns for American goods in Asia fail to capture consumer attention because they are too direct in their appeal or are too boastful. Advertising directors back in the United States often select themes and ideas for these campaigns that do not take into account the importance to Asians of subtlety, indirection, and modesty. Sometimes an idiomatic or humorous expression creeps into the advertising that makes sense to an American but completely escapes the understanding of an Asian. Even worse, sometimes these campaigns employ sexual imagery or some other device that is genuinely offensive to Asians.

Sometimes there are simple translation errors. Billboards for Coca-Cola in China, intending to say "Enjoy Coke" in Chinese, once said "Feel Coke." Not precisely the message intended. One is reminded of the classic and costly error once made by General Motors in marketing its Nova automobile in Latin America; *no vá* means "it will not go" in Spanish.

Such advertising lapses occur on both sides of the cultural divide. A few years ago, Nissan Motors mounted an advertising campaign in the United States for its new Infiniti automobile. On television, the campaign started with a series of beautifully filmed scenes of running water, forests, and other natural subjects, each commercial concluding simply with the word "Infiniti." The television ads were Asian in their quiet elegance and subtlety and much admired by advertising professionals. However, the final assessment was that their indirectness made them ineffective with the American viewing public.

Presentation also has cultural implications. When asked recently what is the most common failing of American companies in introducing products to Japan, the head of a large Japanese trading company quickly responded, "It's amazing how often you see poor packaging." He went on to say, charitably, that Americans often fail to make allowances for the Japanese obsession with harmony and precision.

## DISTRIBUTION BARRIERS

Years ago, at the beginning of the so-called "Green Revolution," when visionaries saw an end to world hunger through higher levels of agricultural production, American fertilizer producers were excited by the prospect of increased sales in poor, overpopulated countries. They soon learned, however, that it is one thing to off-load products from ship to dock in a port city and quite another thing to get those products to the inland areas where they are needed, where roads are narrow or nonexistent.

American exporters of products to Asia need to pay close attention to distribution issues. Physical problems of getting products to market still exist in Asia, especially in large and less developed countries such as China, Indonesia, and the Philippines. Depending on the product marketed, the problems can involve the location and adequacy of deep water ports, rail and highway systems, airports, transportation equipment, and availabiity/accessibility of warehousing facilities.

There also are non-physical, "structural" distribution problems. Japan's distribution systems are clogged by various inefficiencies and exclusive trading relationships. Although Japan has less than half the population of the United States, it has twice the number of wholesalers and retailers. Of course, each tier in the distribution adds time to delivery and cost to the product. These systems are embedded in the social fabric of the country and will not change soon. Similar structural impediments exist in Korea (although the role of wholesalers is not as great) and elsewhere in Asia.

## THROUGH LOCAL EYES AND CONNECTIONS

Such marketing, advertising, and distribution problems are additional reasons for American exporters to seek the help of a local partner or obtain other local advice and representation in Asia.

In Japan, if a local partner is not taken, the help of a Japanese trading company is highly recommended. In Korea, trading agencies provide similar services. Elsewhere in Asia help is always available, some of it excellent, some not worth much. Again, Americans should utilize their networks to identify potential partners, advisors, and representatives, and then make their selections with great care.

Local partners, advisors, and representatives can also be helpful in dealing with several special problem areas.

# Chapter 8

# Special Problem Areas

A vast array of trade barriers exists in most countries of the world in the form of tariffs, quotas, licensing requirements, and various structural impediments. As trade barriers go, those of Asian countries are not prohibitively high. Barriers in Hong Kong and Singapore are quite low because the economies of these two countries depend on free trade. Less developed countries like Indonesia protect domestic industries with high tariffs, but barriers are lowered or eliminated as their economies grow stronger.

Countries like Japan and Korea are known for their structural barriers, such as cumbersome distribution systems and interlocking business relationships that tend to exclude foreign competition. In addition, there are the following special trade issues that American exporters may need to address.

**INTELLECTUAL PROPERTY PROTECTION**

The most serious trade problem in Asia for many American exporters is weak intellectual property protection: i.e., the failure of a country to protect, through its laws and law enforcement systems, the copyrights, trademarks, and patents of foreign and domestic firms alike. In recent years, this was especially true of Korea, Taiwan, China, and Thailand. Visitors to those countries were able to buy designer clothing, Louis Vuitton handbags, Rolex watches, and computer software packages at incredibly low prices. The prices were low because the products were illegally copied by local manufacturers who paid no royalties or license fees to the intellectual property owners.

The problem still exists throughout Asia. Part of the problem in several countries is that Confucian philosophy holds that intellectual properties are "free goods" to be shared by everyone. Indeed, copying is often thought to be a way of showing respect and honor. In addition, although there are now adequate intellectual property laws on the books of most Asian countries, the laws are not adequately enforced and the bureaucratic processes for registering patents, copyrights, and trademarks are not timely. Computer software is especially vulnerable to theft, because it is valuable and easily copied and marketed.

Accordingly, American exporters of virtually any protectable product need to devote considerable attention and vigilance to its protection. This will involve early steps to register property rights, continued monitoring in the marketplace, and aggressive action to enforce one's rights when they are infringed. Some protection also can be gained from contractual arrangements that place the burden, including damages for loss, on local partners. Another source of protection is having highly placed political connections that can activate legal processes or pressure violators into compliance. Here again the local partner's influence could be helpful.

## CUSTOMS AND LICENSING PROCEDURES

Delays in customs clearances and import licensing are often a problem in Asia, especially in the less developed countries. This is because of complex regulations, bureaucratic inefficiencies, and language differences. Packaging, labeling, and testing requirements all add to the difficulties. (In a broad and general sense, the bureaucracy tends to work more efficiently in countries formerly colonized by the British; Singapore, Malaysia, and Hong Kong as prime examples. While such colonization has been regarded as a mixed blessing by many, it is accepted that a positive benefit from that period is an infrastructure that works).

Thailand's reputation in this area is poor. China's complex regulations and bureaucracy frequently cause delays. Indonesia, on the other hand, improved its procedures markedly in 1985 by retaining the Swiss surveying firm Société Générale de Surveillance to inspect shipments arriving in Indonesia and at various points of origin throughout the world.

Depending on the country of destination, American exporters should expect delays and inefficiencies in getting their products into Asia. Again, the careful selection of partners and representatives can do much to expedite the process.

## EXPEDITING PAYMENTS AND INFLUENCE PEDDLING

In a few Asian countries, especially Indonesia, Thailand, and the Philippines, it is common for officials at lower levels of government to expect extra payments ("expediting payments") from anyone requesting them to carry out, or to refrain from carrying out, their responsibilities. For example, imported goods are often not cleared by customs until a customs official receives something of value from an importer, and a licensing infraction sometimes becomes a legal prosecution unless a court official is paid to overlook it. Similarly, various permits and contracts seem never to materialize unless payments are made to a person of influence. These practices occur to some extent in all of the countries featured in this guide with the exception of Japan, Singapore, and Malaysia where they are not tolerated.

Americans find it distasteful and awkward to deal with expediting payments and influence peddling. Many Americans remember the scandals that surfaced during the Watergate investigations involving large payments made by American corporations to influence the actions of foreign governments. One such payment was $3 million paid by Gulf Oil Corporation in 1966 to South Korea's Democratic Republican Party to influence the award of oil exploration concessions. The U.S. law that resulted from those scandals, the Foreign Corrupt Practices Act, now prohibits U.S. corporations and their affiliates from making payments (directly or indirectly) to officials and political parties of foreign governments except to encourage them to perform their normal duties.

Influence peddling and expediting payments occur in many countries throughout the world. Asia is no exception. In some cases, substantial fees are paid to highly placed individuals who serve as "consultants" and "representatives" but do little else than fix things or make things happen. In Taiwan, for example, a "squeeze" of five to ten percent of a transaction's value is often paid to persons or organizations who perform such services.

To the extent that these practices are not illegal but merely distasteful, Americans should accept them as local cultural customs, as indeed they are where they exist in Asia. They are part of the Asian tradition of paying deference to one's superiors (even lowly bureaucrats are considered superior since they represent the government), honoring important personal relationships, and spreading the wealth. Low salaries also play a part. It is an accepted premise in these countries that civil servants derive a portion of their compensation from such payments, not unlike the premise in the United States that waitresses and taxi drivers derive a portion of their compensation from tips.

To avoid frustration and guilt, Americans can best leave matters like these to their local partners and representatives, who in any event, let us assume, provide entirely legitimate and useful services.

# PART II

# Chapter 9

# Country Profiles

Part II of this guide is devoted to profiles of the ten countries that are fueling the Asian economic boom. Incorporated in each profile is a host of specific, practical information concerning the country, its business practices and customs, and its trade opportunities.

Each country profile begins with a story about an American company that is succeeding in Asia. The profile then provides essential business information about the country under the following subject headings:

**Subject Headings**

Economic Background
Language
Religion
Vital Economic Statistics
Best Export Opportunities For American Firms
Business Practices:
    Meetings
    Business Hours
    Greetings
    Business Cards
    Names and Titles
    Clothing
    Gifts and Entertainment
    Conversation
    Hotels
    Exercise
    Transportation and Communications
    Special Considerations
Entry Requirements
Money
Tipping
Major Holidays
Useful Phrases
Useful Contacts

A few brief observations can be made at the outset.

**Making Preparations**

A common theme of this guide is that Americans should prepare carefully for their trips to Asia and should be sensitive to the individual cultures of the countries they visit. Preparations normally require introductions through an intermediary for meetings with Asian organizations.

Presentation materials should be forwarded in advance, if possible. Asians should be carefully advised of the name and position of each American visitor. If a spouse is accompanying an American visitor for business or pleasure, the Asians should be advised.

After arrival in an Asian country, Americans can well use weekends and time between meetings to expand their knowledge of the country and its culture. A city bus tour on a weekend is a good way to start. Bookstores often have interesting English-language publications that one could never find in the United States. Conversations with people in shops, restaurants, and hotels also provide good learning opportunities.

The following four charts provide an overall economic comparison of our ten featured countries in terms of recent growth rates, incomes per capita, and trade positions with the United States.

# GROSS DOMESTIC PRODUCT
## (1991 Estimates)

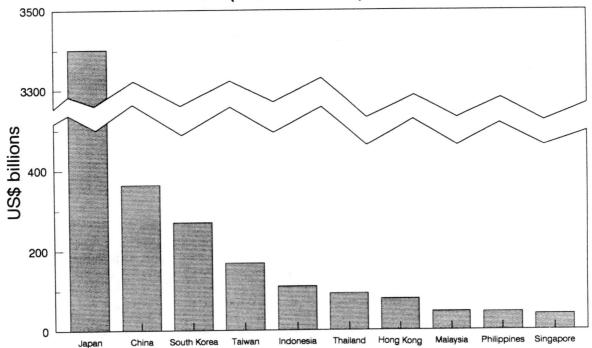

# INCOME PER CAPITA
## (1991 Estimates)

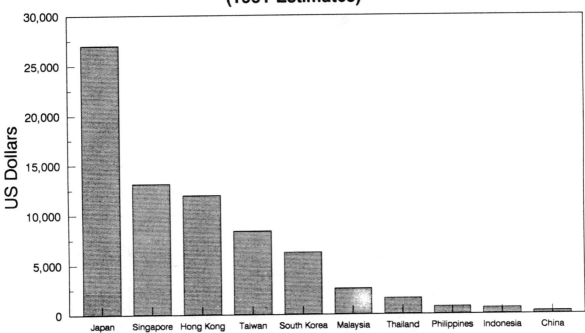

Source:
U.S. Department of Commerce

# IMPORTS FROM THE UNITED STATES
### (As a Percent of Total Manufactured Imports)
### (1991 Estimates)

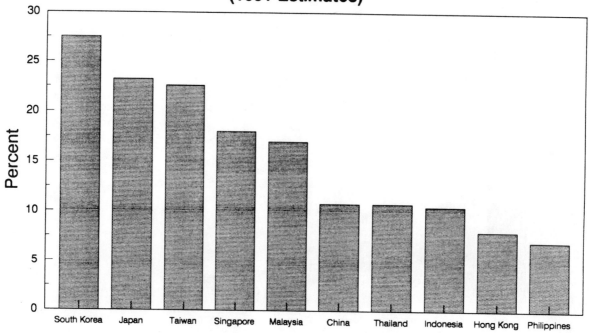

# EXPORTS TO THE UNITED STATES
### (As a Percent of Total Exports)
### (1991 Estimates)

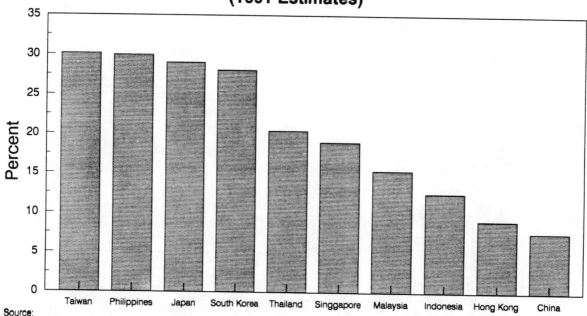

Source:
U.S. Department of Commerce

# COUNTRY PROFILE: CHINA

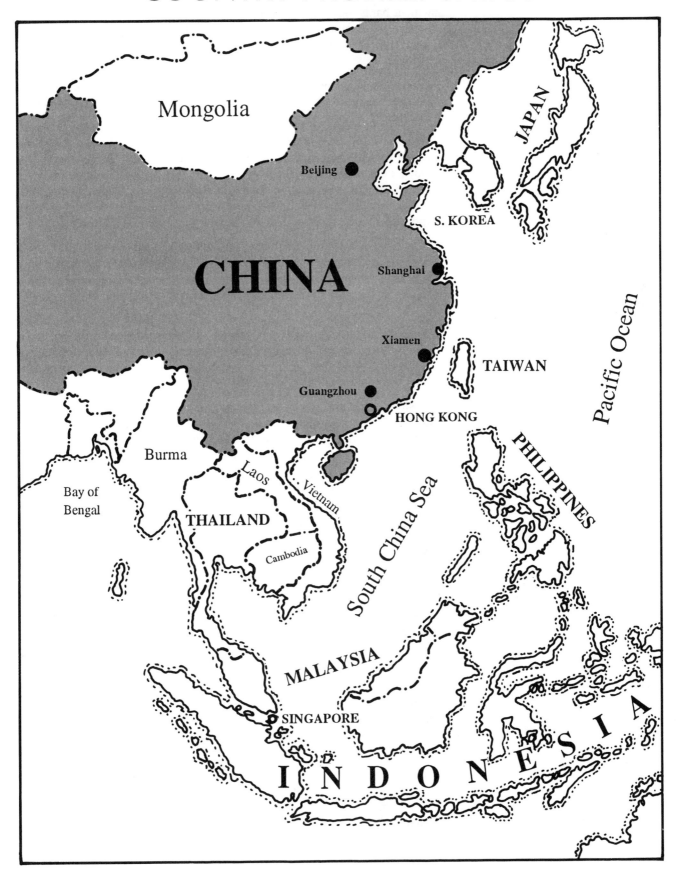

## AN AMERICAN IN CHINA

Charley's Ice Cream Parlour in Beijing near Tiananmen Square serves ice cream cones and related goodies to about 2,000 customers a day, seven days a week, from 9 a.m. to 10 p.m. Charley's literally started with a bang — it was preparing for its opening when the Tiananmen Square pro-democracy demonstrations took place (Charley's opened on June 10, 1989), and there are bullet holes in one of its walls as a reminder.

There are now four Charley's Ice Cream Parlours in China. Besides Beijing, there are Charley's Parlours in Chengdu, Urumqi, and Hainan.

They are the work of Charles K. C. Chang, an American entrepreneur, attorney, and real estate investor who lives in Honolulu. On a trip to China in 1988, Chang was impressed that the Chinese consumed so much ice cream of poor quality. "Over 500,000 tons of ice cream are consumed annually in Shanghai alone," says Chang. "Chocolate, strawberry, and vanilla are the only flavors produced, and the cream content is only about six percent, compared to ten percent or more in the United States."

"I saw an opportunity for these parlours in China," says Chang. "The Chinese are fascinated with American things, they love ice cream, and they need a place to go where they can sit down and have an inexpensive treat. Young couples especially. Our Beijing parlour seats 100 and has a fast turnover. It's almost always busy."

"It took me about a year to work out the first import licenses," adds Chang, "but the Chinese officials were encouraging. They wanted a better quality of life for people in China, and in their minds that included a better quality of ice cream."

To start a Charley's Ice Cream Parlour, Chang typically takes a local partner and works out a lease with the local community organization, called a *danwei*. He then imports ice cream machines from the United States through Hong Kong (where he gets a better price). Finally, he supervises the installation of the machines and the training of employees. (There are about 25 employees in Beijing and ten in each of the other cities.)

"We attribute our success in large part to having twelve great flavors imported from the United States," says Chang. "Chocolate, strawberry, and vanilla cones are readily available on the streets for one yuan. We charge three yuan (about US$.60) and have no trouble making sales."

According to Chang, Americans need to be very flexible and pragmatic in setting up business arrangements with the Chinese. "They're very sharp. You have to be a good negotiator, and you have to know the value of things because the deals are not straightforward. In particular, you have to watch out for inflated prices. When the Chinese see an American coming, they think they're going to get rich."

Also, in joint ventures with Chinese, Americans need to be careful that profits are not maximized at the expense of quality, says Chang. "I often have to remind my Chinese partners to maintain the agreed percentage of cream in our product and to put more effort into cleaning and maintenance."

Another issue for businesses that sell products to local Chinese is the repatriation of profits. It is difficult to convert the local currency, renminbi, into foreign exchange. "But that will change someday," says Chang. "In the meantime, I am reinvesting profits and building the business in China."

**CHINA:
ECONOMIC BACKGROUND**

China (the People's Republic of China) is a salesman's dream. A market of over one billion people. "If each person would just buy one widget ..."

In land area, China is large. It is the third largest country in the world (after Russia and Canada) and is slightly larger than the United States. In terms of population—about 1.2 billion people—China is huge. One fifth of the world's people. More than four times the population of the United States.

Eighty percent of China's people live in the coastal regions of the country (to the east and south) and in the basins of the country's two great rivers, the Yellow and the Yangtze. Its principal commercial cities are Beijing (the capital), Shanghai, Xiamen, Shenzhen, and Guangzhou. First-time American visitors to these cities will be overwhelmed by the numbers of people that swell the streets. These are safe cities, however, and the Chinese are accommodating to visitors.

China is one of the greatest civilizations of all time, having contributed significantly to art, science, and philosophy over the centuries, with recorded history commencing over 3,000 years ago. Feudal dynasties and an imperial system prevailed until 1911 when the Manchu Dynasty came to an end and a republican system began to develop. Political factions contended for power from the early 1920s until civil war erupted in 1945 between the Nationalist Party under Chiang Kai-shek and the Communist Party under Mao Zedong. The Communists won that war, and the Nationalists moved their government to Taiwan.

A centrally planned socialist government and economy then prevailed for the following two decades. A strong industrial base, following the Soviet Union model, was developed during this time. A period of isolation and anti-intellectualism, dubbed the "Cultural Revolution," then brought on disintegration and stagnation of China's social and productive systems during the ten years from 1966 to 1976. Following this, China entered a period of modernization, economic reform, and gradual opening to international trade, a period that continues to the present.

The progress of China's economy since reforms were introduced in 1978 has been remarkable at times. The challenge for the planners is to modulate growth, to smooth the swings between boom and recession. Steps taken in 1988 to cool an overheated economy resulted in a recession in 1988-1989. Growth recently was a manageable six percent. The striking statistic is that China's private sector has strongly outpaced growth in the state-owned and collective sectors. In 1990, for example, output of the private sector grew by 21.6 percent compared to the others' 2.9 percent and 9.1 percent.

During the 1980s, China established a number of economic zones, called Special Economic Zones, Development Zones, and Open Economic Zones, to promote trade and foreign investment. These zones, situated in the coastal and southern provinces of the country, now play an important role in China's economic growth. They provide various tax incentives, tariff concessions, and reduced costs of land and labor. They also facilitate technology transfer, joint ventures, and research projects.

There are three principal problems facing Americans who would export products and services to China. First, China has a low per capita income. The people do not have much to spend. Second, China's infrastructure is poor. Getting goods into the distribution system, to the extent there is one, is an immense task. Transportation systems and communications are poor. Third, China is not a homogeneous market. Its provinces differ in many ways. Therefore, marketing strategies cannot be applied across the board.

On the political side, there are two factors that should be monitored by American exporters to China. The first is continuation of Most-Favored-Nation treatment of China by the United States government. MFN treatment accords to a number of U.S. trading partners various reduced tariffs on exports to the United States and certain other trade concessions. If the United States withdraws MFN for China, China's trade barriers to American exports will surely increase.

The second political factor that American exporters need to monitor is China's leadership succession. Deng Xiaoping, China's paramount leader since 1978, and many of his close associates, are now in their eighties. It is not yet clear to whom China's reins of power will be passed. If the process does not go smoothly, China's international relations and trade could be severely disrupted.

## NEAR-TERM OUTLOOK

China's "faster, bolder" economic reforms, introduced by Deng Xiaoping in 1992 and endorsed by China's Politburo, will energize its Special Economic Zones, notably in Guangdong Province adjacent to Hong Kong. China will play an expanding role in the affairs of Hong Kong prior to 1997 but will not extinguish the flames of capitalism and entrepreneurship there. Stock markets in several Chinese cities will continue to be very popular and well attended, helping to fuel growth.

In the face of strong economic growth, the government will continue efforts to cool demand and restrain inflation. Money supply will be tightly controlled, lending ceilings of banks will be kept low, and government capital spending will be curtailed. These efforts will succeed in holding inflation under 8 percent. Nonetheless, industrial output will grow by at least 10 percent in 1993, and export/import growth will exceed 15 percent.

## LANGUAGE

Mandarin is the official language of China, but there are many dialects, the principal ones being Cantonese, Wu (Shanghai), Fukienese, and Hakka. The written language is ideographic (kanji symbols) and is uniform throughout China.

English is spoken by some but not many.

## RELIGION

China is officially atheist, but its constitution allows freedom of religious belief, and there are Buddhists, Taoists, Muslims, and others. Also, there are a few Christian churches and Islamic mosques in the major cities.

## VITAL ECONOMIC STATISTICS (1991 Estimates)

| | |
|---|---|
| Population: | 1.2 billion |
| Gross Domestic Product | US$ 364 billion |
| Income Per Capita | US$ 314 |
| Annual Growth Rate | 6 percent |
| Total Imports | US$ 57 billion |
| Total Exports | US$ 72 billion |
| U.S. Share of Manufactured Imports | 10.8 percent |
| U.S. Share of Total Exports | 7.6 percent |

**Top Five Imports From U.S.**
Aircraft and parts
Fertilizers
Wheat
Cotton textile fibers
Measuring and scientific instruments

**Top Five Exports To U.S.**
Toys, games, sporting goods
Footwear
Apparel
Trunks, suitcases, briefcases
Crude oil

**Top Three Foreign Investors**
Hong Kong
U.S.
Japan

**Top Three Trading Partners**
Hong Kong
Japan
U.S.

## BEST EXPORT OPPORTUNITIES FOR AMERICAN FIRMS*

**Aircraft and Aircraft Parts**
Wide-body jet aircraft, 100- to 200-passenger jets, parts

**Agricultural Chemicals**
Hi-grade (urea) nitrogen fertilizer, potassium and phosphate fertilizers, selective pesticides

**Industrial Chemicals**
Performance (specialty/fine/proprietary) chemicals, cigarette filter tow

**Yarns**
Cotton yarns, synthetic yarn filaments, synthetic staple fibers, wool/animal hair yarns

**Oil and Gas Field Machinery and Services**
Oil and gas equipment and services, offshore production equipment and services, major pipeline projects, geophysical instruments and secondary recovery equipment

**Computers and Peripherals**
Workstations, 386/486 PCs, printers, networking products

**Chemical Production Machinery**
Process technology (petrochemical and other), petrochemical plants

**Plastic Materials and Resins**
Engineered plastics/composites for consumer and industrial goods

**Mining Industry Equipment**
Open pit mining equipment (trucks, power shovels, etc.), boring and sinking machinery and parts, parts for derricks

**Telecommunications Equipment**
Cellular equipment, satellite earth stations, PBX, digital c.o. switches

---

* U.S. Department of Commerce 1992 Rankings

| | |
|---|---|
| **Automotive Parts and Service Equipment** | Special purpose vehicles' parts/accessories (e.g., for concrete mixing, freight, oil tank, chemical, garbage, ambulance, and other such vehicles), auto and motorcycle parts/accessories (e.g., air conditioners, rear axle components, special new/luxury equipment) |
| **Laboratory Scientific Instruments** | Industrial instruments, scientific instruments |
| **Power Transmission Equipment** | Transformers, switchgear, cable and related equipment (towers/insulators) |
| **Plastics Production Machinery** | Packaging materials |
| **Electric Power Systems** | Steam turbines, boilers, control/communication/monitoring systems, gas turbine generators |
| **Avionics and Ground Support Equipment** | Navigational aids, radio/radar equipment, communications equipment |
| **Pumps, Valves, and Compressors** | For chemical plants, petrochemical plants, oil and gas |
| **CAD/CAM/CAE/CIM** | (Computer Assisted Design/Manufacturing/Engineering; Computer Integrated Manufacturing) Graphic workstations, high resolution monitors, CAD/CAM software |
| **Medical Equipment** | CT scanners, disposable syringes |
| **Pollution Control Equipment** | Equipment for water, air, waste, and noise pollution control |
| **Electronics Production and Test Equipment** | Electron beam equipment, ion implanters, SMT production equipment, oscilloscopes |
| **Paper and Paperboard** | Uncoated and unbleached kraft liner, wastepaper, newsprint |
| **Machine Tools and Metalworking Equipment** | Parts for rolling mills, casting machinery, machining centers for metalworking, high precision/efficiency machine tools, n/c systems, hydraulic systems, measuring instruments, forging/foundry equipment, heavy duty machine tools |
| **Computer Software and Services** | Operating system software, database management software, network software, specialized applications |
| **Construction Equipment** | Dump trucks, large earth-moving equipment, road paving equipment |
| **Building Products** | Specialty woods/plywoods, float glass, auto safety glass, specialty cements, tiles |

| | |
|---|---|
| **Process Controls—Industrial** | Power plant instrumentation, chemical plant/refinery process controls |
| **Port and Shipbuilding Equipment** | Small 30- to 80-hp all-wheel drive loaders, large fork lifts for container handling, coal handling equipment, harbor traffic control systems |
| **Materials Handling Equipment** | Conveying systems, storage systems, lift trucks |
| **Electronic Components** | 80386 chip sets, other microprocessors, D-RAM |
| **Textile Machinery** | HS 84819 auxiliary machinery for textile machines, textile finishing machinery, knitting machinery, textile spinning machines |
| **Architectural, Construction, and Engineering Services** | Services for power stations, subways, ports, transportation (roads and railways) |
| **Drugs and Pharmaceuticals** | Antibiotics, specialty medicines |
| **Food Processing and Packaging Equipment** | Baby foods, food packaging equipment, freezing/cold storage equipment, pasteurizing/sterilizing equipment |
| **Railroad Equipment** | Signaling equipment, special rail inspection cars, consulting services |
| **Agricultural Machinery** | Grain storage facilities, large grain combines, haying equipment, pesticides |
| **Packaging Equipment** | Packaging for agricultural products and bulk materials such as cement, high speed boxing and sealing lines for consumer products destined for export markets |
| **Pulp and Paper Machinery** | Machinery for making bags and envelopes, machinery to help improve/expand China's particleboard sector, pulping equipment, second-hand equipment for treating wastepaper, modern and high speed equipment for making hygienic paper, cigarette paper, and paper for making color film |
| **Water Resources Equipment** | Irrigation equipment, municipal water supply upgrades |
| **Printing, Graphics** | Print type and blocks, parts for machinery/equipment to make print blocks, machines and parts for uses ancillary to printing |
| **Dental Equipment** | Dental drills, parts and accessories, dental instruments |

## BUSINESS PRACTICES

### Meetings

Appointments must be arranged well in advance. Often the proper protocol is for the Chinese host to issue a written invitation to meet, rather than merely agree to meet.

Punctuality is important.

### Business Hours

The Chinese normally work a six-day week, Monday through Saturday. Hours are from 8 a.m. to 6 p.m., with an hour and a half to two hours taken at noon.

### Greetings

A slight bow is customary, but shaking hands is now common in business settings.

### Business Cards

Don't be caught without them. They are very important in introductions and in starting meetings off on the right foot. Be sure that your title indicates your responsibilities or be prepared to do a lot of explaining. (For example, the Chinese might understand "Manager of Production" but not "Director of Communications.") The card should be printed in Chinese on one side.

### Names and Titles

The surname always comes first in China, an indication of the cultural importance of the family. Accordingly, Mao was Mao Zedong's "last" name.

Titles are important in China, and Americans should use titles when addressing important Chinese in formal surroundings. For example, when addressing Manager of Production Li Qing, one should say, "Manager Li." On social occasions, however, one should simply say, "Mr. Li."

Chinese women do not take their husband's names. If married, they should be addressed with their title, if they have one, or "Madame" if the title is not known. If they have no title, use "Miss" (even though married) or "Mrs." ("Ms." is not used in China.)

### Clothing

Suits and ties, of darker colors, are the most appropriate apparel for men. In warm weather, however, shirt-sleeves, without jackets and ties, are acceptable. Also, jackets may be doffed and ties loosened in meetings and at banquets when comfort calls.

Business suits (skirts or pants) are the proper attire for women, too. American business women should be sparing in their use of jewelry and cosmetics.

### Gifts and Entertainment

Gifts are important in China, as they are throughout Asia. However, owing to Communist ideology and official disapproval of materialism and excess, gifts should not be lavish or personal. Rather, they should be thoughtful and should be bestowed, nominally at least, upon the recipient's organization. Gifts to the leader or ranking members of the Chinese organization with which you are dealing are the best bet.

Banquets are popular in China. Your Chinese host may host a banquet in your honor, and you will be expected to reciprocate before returning to the United States. You will find that the guest lists for such occasions can be lengthy.

The Chinese normally do not entertain foreign visitors in their homes.

**Conversation** Avoid political discussions and any criticism of government leadership and policies. And it will not reflect well on you if you criticize your own government. China should be referred to as "China" or "the People's Republic of China," not "Mainland China." Taiwan should be referred to as the "Province of Taiwan," not (as Taiwan calls itself) "the Republic of China."

Good topics of conversation include Chinese culture and history, the abilities of China's athletes at the Olympics, various American lifestyles, and your own personal interests. The Chinese do not hesitate to ask personal questions, so be prepared to disclose your age, your income, and the details of your family life.

**Hotels** Reserve well in advance, especially if your stay will include a national holiday.

Stay in one of the better Western-style hotels. The alternatives are unsatisfactory for American business people, and there is no advantage to "going native."

**Exercise** You'll enjoy jogging or taking long walks or joining groups of Chinese doing early morning *tai chi*, the ballet-like martial arts exercise that limbers body and mind. To try *tai chi*, just look for a nearby park, stand towards the back of a group doing the exercises, and follow their motions.

Athletic wear, including shorts, is acceptable attire for men and women.

**Transportation and Communications** If your Chinese hosts do not arrange local transportation for you, you might want to hire a car and driver or take a taxi. Taxis are not plentiful, however, or easily hailed. Buses, trains, and domestic flights are very crowded.

Telephones are not as prevalent in China as they are in the United States, nor do they work very well. However, hotels and many offices have modern telephone equipment and fax machines. Plan to do your local and international telephoning and faxing from your hotel or your host's offices.

**Special Considerations** China is a Communist country. Although a private sector is emerging, Americans will encounter attitudes and practices that are markedly different from their own. Moreover, many of the persons with whom Americans will deal, even in business, are essentially government bureaucrats.

Gaining access to foreign technology is a high priority for China. This presents good opportunities to American firms for licensing and joint ventures. However, intellectual property protection in China is presently poor, and Americans need to take steps to protect their technology and know-how or obtain adequate compensation for it in transactions with Chinese. Contractual protections help to some degree but not with respect to third parties who gain access to one's technology.

China also needs management skills. This presents many opportunities to American firms that can supply management know-how and systems to the Chinese under contract or in joint ventures with them.

Joint ventures with Hong Kong organizations that do business in China are a good way for American firms to approach China's markets.

In gifts, packaging, and promotional materials, Americans should avoid yellow (the color of emperors) and purple (the color of barbarians). Do not give clocks as gifts (the word in Chinese sounds like a word relating to funerals, and they are symbols of bad luck), and do not wrap gifts in white which also signifies funerals and bad luck.

If you display a map, be certain that Hong Kong and Taiwan are not identified as independent countries.

## ENTRY REQUIREMENTS

Americans on business need a passport, an official invitation from a sponsor in China, a visa, sufficient funds for the stay, and a ticket and documents for onward travel.

## MONEY

"People's currency," known as the yuan, is issued by the People's Bank of China. The principal denomination is the yuan. The cost of things is expressed in yuan; for example, "That will be 20 yuan."

The yuan is issued in two forms: FEC (Foreign Exchange Currency) and RMB (Renminbi). FEC is accepted by most hotels, restaurants, shops, and taxis. RMB is a parallel currency used by the Chinese people but having no exchange value outside China. Americans should use only FEC.

Major credit cards are accepted at establishments catering to international visitors. Cash (FEC) may be obtained at banks and major hotels. International travelers checks are normally accepted at larger establishments throughout China.

One U.S. dollar is equal to about five and a half yuan.

## TIPPING

Tipping offends the Chinese, so do not tip. If services have been especially thoughtful and personal, express your appreciation verbally or with a small gift, such as a packet of postcards with pictures of United States scenes.

## MAJOR HOLIDAYS

| | |
|---|---|
| New Year's Day | January 1 |
| Chinese New Year | Late January or early February |
| Labor Day | May 1 |
| National Day | October 1 |

## USEFUL PHRASES

| English | Chinese Pinyin* | Phonetic Pronunciation |
|---|---|---|
| Hello | Ni hao | Knee how |
| Good morning | Zao shang hao | Tzaow shang how |
| Good evening | Wan shang hao | Wahn shang how |
| Good night | Wan an | Wahn ahn |
| Good-bye | Zai jian | Dzye jee-en |
| Yes | Dui | Doo-ee |
| No | Bu dui | Boo doo-ee |
| Please | Qing | Ching |

\*  Mandarin

| English | Chinese Pinyin | Phonetic Pronunciation |
|---|---|---|
| How much? | Duo shao | Doo-oh shah-oh |
| Thank you | Xie xie | Shee-yeh shee-yeh |
| You're welcome | Bu xie | Boo shee-yeh |
| Cheers | Gan bei | Kahm pie |
| I don't understand | Wo bu dong | Wah boo dong |

## USEFUL CHINA CONTACTS

China Council for Promotion of International Trade
1 Fu Xing Men Wai Jie
Beijing, 100860
The People's Republic of China
TELEPHONE: 86*/1-801-3344
FAX: 86 -1-801-1370

China Council for Promotion of International Trade
4301 Connecticut Avenue, N.W.
Washington, DC 20008
TELEPHONE: 202/244-3244
FAX: 202/244-0478

All-China Federation of Industry and Commerce
93 Beiheyan Dajie
Beijing, 100006
The People's Republic of China
TELEPHONE: 86-1-513-6677
FAX: 86-1-512-2631

U. S. Embassy
Commercial Section
Xiu Shui Bei Jie 3
Jianguomenwai
Beijing, 100600
The People's Republic of China
TELEPHONE: 86-1-532-3831
FAX: 86-1-532-3297

The United States-China Business Council
CITIC Building
Beijing, 100004
The People's Republic of China
TELEPHONE: 86-1-500-2255
FAX: 86-1-512-5854

The United States-China Business Council
1818 N Street, N.W.
Washington, DC 20036
TELEPHONE: 202/429-0340
FAX: 202/775-2476

* China's country code

# COUNTRY PROFILE: HONG KONG

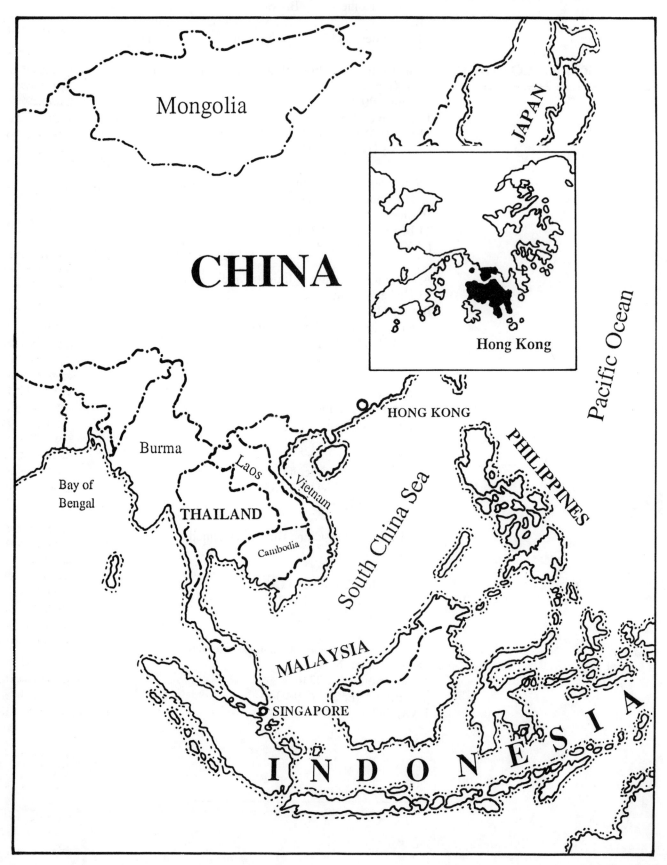

## OPENING DOORS IN HONG KONG

When he was growing up in the small town of Sparta, Tennessee, David Goff had no idea that years later he would be making a substantial impact on the lives of people on the other side of the world.

Today Goff is Director of Sales and Marketing of Shaffield Industries of Sparta, a manufacturer of premium hardwood furniture. A classic American example of entrepreneurial success, Shaffield was started by brothers Bill and Gary Shaffield during their high school years in the late 1960s, when they began staining lacrosse sticks in the basement of their home as subcontractors for a local manufacturing company. Shaffield now manufactures a broad line of wood products, mostly furniture. It employs about 100 people and occupies about 200,000 square feet of manufacturing and warehousing facilities in Sparta. Its annual sales are over $15 million.

In July 1991, Goff and executives of twelve other small businesses traveled to Taiwan and South Korea on a U.S. government sponsored "Matchmaker" trade mission for manufacturers of U.S. consumer products. Commercial officers of the U.S. Department of Commerce arranged appointments in each country with prospective buyers and distributors.

As a side benefit of his exposure to Taiwan and Korea, Goff also saw Hong Kong as another good market for Shaffield products, and subsequently made three trips there to call on potential distributors.

On each of his trips, Goff carried with him colorful brochures and photographs of Shaffield's "From The Source" line of premium futons and futon furniture frames. Interest in the products was strong. Shaffield also exhibited in the Taipei Furniture Show February 1992, and Goff further developed and expanded his contacts.

"The market is wide open for our products," says Goff. He explains that Asians love wood products and find it prestigious to own them. Premium wood products are not widely available in Hong Kong, Korea, and Taiwan.

"Tenacity is very important," says Goff. "We were interested in dealing with a certain stocking distributor in Hong Kong, one who supplies large department stores. On my third visit to this person, he said, 'You have been very persistent. Let's do business together.' He immediately picked up the phone and arranged for me to see two department store buyers. We are now working with this distributor on a continuing basis."

One of the most critical initial steps for an American exporter to Asia, according to Goff, is the selection of one or more distributors. You need to be sure that the distributor's business objectives and marketing approach are compatible with yours, that you feel you can trust the people you are dealing with, and that the firm is adequately financed. "It's like hiring a key employee," Goff says. "You check him out, you try to get to know him, you make your best judgment call, and you hope it works out."

When he was looking for distributors in Hong Kong, South Korea, and Taiwan, he uncovered plenty of candidates, says Goff. "Many wanted an exclusive arrangement and wanted to know our best price." Presently Shaffield has one distributor in Hong Kong, two in Taiwan, and one in South Korea. The Japanese market also looks especially attractive to them, and they expect to establish a representation office in Tokyo in the near future.

What problems lie ahead? Shaffield is aware that its products and designs can be copied in Asia. To counter this, they are taking steps to patent some new furniture mechanisms in South Korea, Taiwan, Hong Kong, and Japan. They also plan to maintain their high standards of quality and to establish brand name recognition.

"The market is there," says Goff. "It's all a matter of staying two steps ahead of the competition."

## HONG KONG: ECONOMIC BACKGROUND

Hong Kong is the quintessential city for business. It is considered by many to be the world's foremost international business center, surpassing even London, New York, and Tokyo in all commercial essentials other than financial clout.

An old Hong Kong proverb goes: "Register a business in the morning. Open in the afternoon. Have a profit by nightfall."

Visitors to Hong Kong immediately feel the quick tempo of life there. Business is in the air. Everywhere people are buying, selling, trading, planning, and plotting. While Hong Kong is primarily a trading center, light industry (especially in the New Territories) and financial services have grown steadily in recent years.

Hong Kong is a city of small businesses. However, it does have its huge enterprises, like Jardine Matheson and Hutchinson Whampoa, and it has the regional offices of some of the world's largest multinational corporations. Nevertheless, the great majority of economic activities in Hong Kong are carried out by businesses with less then twenty-five employees. In keeping with a collectivist culture, these businesses are invariably family-owned and family-run.

Hong Kong is also highly entrepreneurial. Sons and daughters and siblings and cousins in family-owned businesses—and many others—are continually striking out on their own to start a new business and "have a profit by nightfall." Competition is keen, and opportunities are seldom overlooked.

Hong Kong consists of Hong Kong Island, Kowloon Peninsula, the New Territories, and a scattering of small islands; in all, about 412 square miles of land area on the southeast coast of China. It has a population of about six million people, including a large expatriate business community. About 30,000 Americans make their livings in Hong Kong.

The commercial history of Hong Kong is surprisingly modern. International commerce did not become active in Hong Kong until the British established it as a Crown Colony in 1841. Hong Kong remained under British administration from that time until the present, except for four years of occupation by the Japanese during World War II.

The future of Hong Kong as a business center is now linked to China. In 1984, the governments of the People's Republic of China and Britain signed a Joint Declaration for the return of Hong Kong to China on July 1, 1997. Hong Kong will then become a Special Administrative Region within China and will retain a high degree of autonomy except in foreign affairs and defense. It will continue to have that status for fifty years, at which time it will come under the direct administration of China.

The Joint Declaration precipitated a capital- and brain-drain in Hong Kong, many fearing that China would dismantle the colony's capitalist institutions. Well-to-do Hong Kongese relocated themselves and their businesses to North America and other parts of the world. Many other talented business people left to seek their fortunes elsewhere.

Recently, however, confidence in the commercial future of Hong Kong has been rebuilding. One reason is that China's own economy has grown tremendously in the years since the Joint Declaration, tilting strongly in free market and private sector directions. (See the China section of this guide.) It also is significant that China has signaled, in various ways, its intention to permit Hong Kong to continue its commercial activities. In particular, in 1991, it approved construction of a new $5.6 billion Hong Kong airport and agreed to other infrastructure improvements.

Perhaps the most critical factor influencing Hong Kong's future is its importance to China as a trading center. Fully forty percent of China's trade now goes through Hong Kong. There is no reason to believe that China will permit this substantial component of its international trade to wither.

## NEAR-TERM OUTLOOK

Confidence in Hong Kong's future will grow in parallel with China's economic growth. Clearly China will take an increasingly active interest in Hong Kong's affairs. It will continue to send signals that it will tolerate Hong Kong's capitalist ways after 1997. Instead of an exodus of business talent from Hong Kong, as there was in the 1980s, there will be a net immigration of skilled and trained personnel. Foreign investment also will rise.

Hong Kong's high-tech industries—electronics for example—will experience strong growth. Such labor intensive industries as textiles and toys will grow more moderately, losing market share to China and other countries with lower wage rates.

Construction of Hong Kong's new airport will fuel demand for engineering and contracting services and capital equipment. Expansion of technology-based industries will boost demand for high-tech services and equipment. Hong Kong's role as a trading center will continue, with many products re-exported (imported for export elsewhere). Aggregate volumes of imports and exports will grow by at least 15 percent in 1993. Strong economic activity is likely to produce an inflation rate of about 11 percent.

## LANGUAGE

English and Chinese—written and spoken—are the two official languages of Hong Kong. English is widely used in commercial and financial circles. Cantonese has been the principal Chinese dialect spoken, but Mandarin is now coming into wider use. The written Chinese language is ideographic (kanji symbols) and is uniform regardless of dialect.

## RELIGION

Hong Kong's principal religions are Buddhism, Taoism, and Christianity. Sizable Muslim, Hindu, and Sikh communities also exist.

## VITAL ECONOMIC STATISTICS (1991 Estimates)

| | |
|---|---|
| Population: | 5.8 million |
| Gross Domestic Product | US$ 79 billion |
| Income Per Capita | US$ 12,000 |
| Annual Growth Rate | 3.6 percent |
| Total Imports | US$ 90.6 billion |
| Total Exports | US$ 90.4 billion |
| U.S. Share of Manufactured Imports | 8 percent |
| U.S. Share of Total Exports | 9.1 percent |

| | |
|---|---|
| **Top Five Imports From U.S.** | Machinery and transport equipment<br>Electrical machinery apparatus and appliances and parts<br>Artificial resins and plastic materials<br>Office machines and automatic data processing equipment<br>Tobacco, manufactured |
| **Top Five Exports To U.S.** | Articles of apparel and clothing accessories<br>Watches and clocks<br>Baby carriages, toys, games, and sporting goods<br>Parts for office/auto data processing machines<br>Telecommunication equipment and parts |
| **Top Three Foreign Investors** | U.S.<br>Japan<br>China |
| **Top Three Trading Partners** | China<br>Japan<br>U.S. |

## BEST EXPORT OPPORTUNITIES FOR AMERICAN FIRMS*

| | |
|---|---|
| **Computers and Peripherals** | Thermal printers, laser printers, information storage and retrieval equipment, and laptop computers |
| **Computer Software and Services** | Software |
| **Architectural, Construction, and Engineering Services** | For a new zoo to be built in the New Territories |
| **CAD/CAM/CAE/CIM** | (Computer Assisted Design/Manufacturing/Engineering; Computer Integrated Manufacturing) |
| **Electronic Components** | Barcoding scanners |
| **Electronics Production and Test Equipment** | PCB equipment |
| **Printing and Graphic Arts Equipment** | Rotary printing presses, parts and components, desk-top publishing systems, modular systems, color separation, pagination and plate making systems |
| **Telecommunications Equipment** | Local area and wide area network equipment, cellular data equipment, CT2 |
| **Pollution Control Equipment** | Hazardous waste removal, water quality control |

* U.S. Department of Commerce 1992 Rankings

| | |
|---|---|
| **Security and Safety Equipment** | Traffic control and safety products, electronic surveillance equipment, alarms and detection apparatus |
| **Avionics and Ground Support Equipment** | Airport ground support equipment, airport instrumentation and equipment |
| **Plastic Materials and Resins** | Acrylonitailebutadiene styrene, high density polyethylene, low density polyethylene, polystyrene |
| **Telecommunications Service** | Satellite telecommunications |
| **Hotel and Restaurant Equipment** | Kitchen equipment |
| **Food Processing and Packaging Equipment** | |
| **Medical Equipment** | Physical therapy equipment, rehabilitation equipment, plastic surgery instruments, diagnostic apparatus |
| **Advertising Services** | Television, print media |
| **Cosmetics and Toiletries** | |
| **Fast food restaurants** | Franchising |
| **Building Products** | Specialty steels, steel cables, concrete large diameter pipe |
| **Construction Equipment** | "Quiet" equipment, tunnel boring machines |
| **Paper and Paperboard** | Newsprint, kraftliner, corrugated paper |
| **Laboratory Scientific Instruments** | Instruments for chemical analysis, electronic automatic regulators, electronic measuring instruments, parts |
| **Travel and Tourism Services** | |
| **Furniture** | Office furniture |
| **Textiles and Fabrics** | Upholstery products, towels and bed sheets |
| **Packaging Equipment** | Packaging equipment for food processing industry |
| **Machine Tools and Metalworking Equipment** | |
| **Management Consulting Services** | |

**Financial Services**

| | |
|---|---|
| **Insurance Services** | General insurance |
| **Audio/Visual Equipment** | Color TVs, Karaoke equipment, laser disk equipment |
| **Drugs and Pharmaceuticals** | Vitamins, penicillin, antibiotics, hormones |
| **Air-conditioning and Refrigeration Equipment** | Split unit air conditioners, no frost refrigerators |
| **Port and Shipbuilding Equipment** | Cargo handling equipment, inventory controls, EDI, parking/storage of trucks and containers |
| **Railroad Equipment** | Fare collection equipment, air-conditioning units, elevators, escalators, safety and security equipment |

## BUSINESS PRACTICES

**Meetings**

Prepare well for any meeting. Appointments normally must be arranged well in advance. Hong Kong trade offices in the United States (see end of this section) will help you with letters of introduction and assist you in making appointments.

Punctuality is important.

**Business Hours**

Monday through Friday, normally from 9 a.m. to 5:30 p.m., with an hour for lunch taken from 1 p.m. to 2 p.m. Some offices are open on Saturday morning.

**Greetings**

A slight bow is customary for the Chinese. Shaking hands is now also common for men and women in business settings.

**Business Cards**

Business cards are always exchanged on first meeting. They are very important in introductions and in starting meetings off on the right foot. Cards need not be printed in Chinese on one side since English is one of Hong Kong's official languages.

**Names and Titles**

Contrary to Chinese tradition, the surnames of Chinese people in Hong Kong (at least those who are in frequent contact with the international business community) often appear last, Western style. For example, Chen Li Meng, whose family name is Chen, is likely to go by the name Li Meng Chen in Hong Kong business circles.

Titles are important in Hong Kong for formal introductions. In other circumstances, "Mr.," "Dr.," "Mrs.," or "Miss" is appropriate. "Ms." is not often used. First names are seldom appropriate.

**Clothing**

Hong Kong dresses on the conservative and formal side. Suits and ties for men, skirts and blouses or dresses for women, but not pantsuits. Dark or muted colors are most common.

**Gifts and Entertainment**    Gifts associated with your organization or your part of the United States are popular, as are fruit, candy and cookies (which you can buy in Hong Kong). (Flowers, however, are not normally appropriate since they are associated with funerals.) Remember that people in Hong Kong have sophisticated tastes.

Hosting a dinner or banquet constitutes an appropriate gift in Hong Kong. This can be easily arranged at one of the city's hotels.

As one might expect in Hong Kong, it is acceptable to mix business with pleasure. Consequently, business discussions are often held during meals, mostly at lunch.

**Conversation**    Because it is such an international city, there are few topics that are out of bounds for conversations in Hong Kong. In speaking with Chinese, however, it is well to keep in mind their collectivist interests in family and social harmony. Political issues, and personal questions relating to Hong Kong's future, are sensitive and probably should be avoided.

Good topics of conversation in Hong Kong will always include business, shopping, and cost of living in Hong Kong and your part of the United States.

**Hotels**    Reserve in advance as you normally would do. Most of the top-rated hotels are conveniently located and provide exceptional service.

**Exercise**    Opportunities for exercise are limited in this crowded city. However, a number of the hotels have exercise facilities, and a dedicated jogger will always find a way to pump up his heart rate. Equally dedicated shoppers also will not lack for exercise.

If you are staying near a park or square, try joining a group of Chinese going through their early morning *tai chi* exercises. Just stand towards the back of a group and follow their motions. Standard athletic wear, including shorts, is acceptable attire for men and women.

**Transportation and Communications**    Transportation in and around Hong Kong is excellent. Trams, buses, and harbor ferries are cheap. There is a modern subway and taxis are convenient and inexpensive. However because this is a heavily populated and very busy area, traffic can be a problem. Allow plenty of time to get where you are going.

Telecommunications also are excellent. Fax machines are in wide use. International direct dialing is available throughout the city, and the postal service is excellent as well. International courier services are widely available.

**Special Considerations**    Avoid the colors blue and white in packaging, promotional materials, and gift wrapping since they are associated with mourning. Popular colors are red, gold, and green.

Hong Kong Chinese tend to be superstitious people. Americans should heed suggestions that a product be introduced, a meeting held, or a contract signed on a certain day or in a certain manner.

**ENTRY REQUIREMENTS**

Americans need their passports, sufficient funds for the stay, and a ticket and documents for onward travel. Visas are required for visits of over 30 days.

**MONEY**

Currency is the Hong Kong dollar, signified by the prefix HK$. Cash is easily obtained at banks and hotels. Major credit cards and international travelers checks are accepted throughout Hong Kong.

One U.S. dollar is equal to about HK$8.

**TIPPING**

Tipping exists but is not prevalent in Hong Kong. Porters, doormen, and others providing special services can be given small cash tips, normally HK$5 per item carried and at least HK$10 when more than one item is carried. Waiters are usually tipped 5 to 10 percent, in addition to the service charge added to your bill. Taxi drivers are given small change. If services have been especially thoughtful and personal during your stay, express your appreciation verbally or with a small gift such as candy.

**MAJOR HOLIDAYS**

| | |
|---|---|
| New Year's Day | January 1 |
| Lunar New Year | Late Jan. or early Feb. |
| Good Friday | Friday before Easter |
| The day following Good Friday | |
| Easter | March/April* |
| Easter Monday | |
| Ching Ming Festival | April |
| Birthday, Queen of England | April 15 |
| Tuen Ng Festival | June |
| Saturday before last Monday in | August |
| Liberation Day | August 26 |
| Day following Mid-Autumn Festival | September |
| Chung Yeung Festival | October |
| Christmas Day | December 25 |
| Boxing Day | December 26 |

**USEFUL PHRASES**

| English | Cantonese** | Phonetic Pronunciation |
|---|---|---|
| Hello | Neih hau | Nay hoe |
| Good morning | Jou sahn | Joe sun |
| Good afternoon | M'an | Mm-on |
| Good night | Jou tau | Joe tow |
| Good-bye | Joi gin | Joy gin |
| Yes | Haih | High |
| No | Mhaih | Mm-high |
| Please | Ching neih | Ching-nay |
| How much? | Geih do tsing | Gay doh tsin |
| Thank you | Do jeh | Doh-jay |
| You're welcome | Mmsaih do jeh | Mm-sigh doh-jay |
| Cheers | Yum tsing | Yum-sin |
| I don't understand | Mming baak | Mm-ing bahk |

---

\*   Date varies
\*\* See China section for Mandarin

**USEFUL HONG KONG CONTACTS**

Hong Kong Government Trade Department
700 Nathan Road
Kowloon, Hong Kong
TELEPHONE: 852*/789-7555
FAX: 852/789-2491

One-Stop Unit
Hong Kong Government Industry Department
Ocean Centre, Canton Road
Kowloon, Hong Kong
TELEPHONE: 852/737-2573
FAX: 852/730-4633

Hong Kong Economic and Trade Office
680 Fifth Avenue
New York, NY 10019
TELEPHONE: 212/265-8888
FAX: 212/974-3209

Hong Kong Economic and Trade Office
180 Sutter Street
San Francisco, CA 94104
TELEPHONE: 415/956-4560
FAX: 415/421-0646

Hong Kong Economic and Trade Office
1233 20th Street
Washington, DC 20036
TELEPHONE: 202/331-8947
FAX: 202/331-8958

Hong Kong Trade Development Council
Convention Plaza, 1 Harbour Road
Hong Kong
TELEPHONE: 852/584-4333
FAX: 852/824-0249

Hong Kong Trade Development Council
333 North Michigan Avenue
Chicago, IL 60601
TELEPHONE: 312/726-4515
FAX: 312/726-2441

Hong Kong Trade Development Council
166 World Trade Center
2050 Stemmons Freeway
Dallas, TX 75207
TELEPHONE: 214/748-8162
FAX: 214/742-6701

* Hong Kong's country code

Hong Kong Trade Development Council
350 South Figueroa Street
Los Angeles, CA 90071
TELEPHONE: 213/622-3194
FAX: 213/613-1490

Hong Kong Trade Development Council
673 Fifth Avenue
New York, NY 10022
TELEPHONE: 212/838-8688
FAX: 212/838-8941

Hong Kong Trade Development Council
Courvoisier Centre
501 Brickell Key Drive
Miami, FL 33131
TELEPHONE: 305/577-0414
FAX: 305/372-9142

U.S. Consulate General
Commercial Section
26 Garden Road, Central
Hong Kong
TELEPHONE: 852/521-1467
FAX: 852/845-9800

The American Chamber of Commerce in Hong Kong
1030 Swire House, Central District
Hong Kong
TELEPHONE: 852/526-0165
FAX: 852/810-1289

Hong Kong Customs and Excise Department
Harbour Building
38 Pier Road, Central
Hong Kong
TELEPHONE: 852/852-1411
FAX: 852/398-0145

# COUNTRY PROFILE: INDONESIA

## CONSULTING IN JAKARTA

"Mike and I were young partners at Touche Ross in Jakarta, and we knew that there were terrific consulting opportunities for Americans who knew their way around Indonesia and Southeast Asia," says James Castle who formed Business Advisory Indonesia with Michael Selby in 1983. "We didn't feel we had to be a branch office of a large American accounting or management consulting firm. In many cases such firms are actually at a disadvantage because they lack flexibility."

At the time, Castle and Selby were doing pioneering work in industrial research, joint venture formation, financial restructuring, and commercial economic forecasting. Castle specialized in industrial research and economic forecasting. Selby was a financial specialist who had structured and managed Indonesia's first multinational leveraged buy-out. Each had assisted in forming numerous multinational joint ventures. "Even though Indonesia was beginning to suffer from the fall of oil prices, we believed that it had a bright future. We knew that it wouldn't be long before Indonesia followed in the footsteps of some of its faster-growing neighbors," says Castle.

Castle and Selby started Business Advisory Indonesia with a professional staff of ten people. Among their first assignments were the formation of a joint venture for Du Pont and a twenty-year economic forecast for Shell Oil. Not long after the firm's formation, the U.S. Agency for International Development (USAID) awarded it a major contract to advise the Indonesian Investment Board on ways to increase the number of American-Indonesian joint ventures. In winning the contract, the firm beat out competition from several well-known international consulting companies.

"We had some lean periods when we were starting out, but we were fortunate to quickly develop several loyal clients," says Castle. "Winning the USAID contract helped our cash flow and really put us on the map. By 1985 we were able to open offices in Bangkok and Singapore, and we've steadily added new offices around the region. We now have offices or representation in Jakarta, Singapore, Bangkok, Kuala Lumpur, Manila, Hong Kong, Sydney, and Seattle."

Business Advisory's clients now include more than 100 of the world's largest companies, numbering among them IBM, Kajima Construction, and Procter & Gamble, and over 50 of Indonesia's largest business groups. Many medium-sized companies, including American firms and a number of Southeast Asian companies also are on the client list.

"There's plenty of room in Asia for American companies—and American consultants—if they do it right," according to Castle.

Business Advisory's Jakarta office handles most of the group's business development services, such as market studies, partner searches, and joint venture structuring. Its Singapore office coordinates the financial and corporate restructuring services. The Jakarta office has been responsible for the introduction, organization, and implementation of more than 50 new business ventures in Indonesia in the past decade.

"We attribute our own success to knowing the languages, cultures, and business practices of the region and to having good working relationships with the region's local business communities and governmental organizations," says Castle.

## INDONESIA: ECONOMIC BACKGROUND

The Spice Islands was an early name for a portion of what is now Indonesia. The days when the cloves, nutmeg, cinnamon, and other spices of this region were the rage of Europe (in the 16th and 17th centuries) are now long gone. Today the spice of Indonesia is in the promise of its bright future.

Rich in human and natural resources, Indonesia is a developing country of tremendous potential. It is the largest of the Southeast Asian countries, a nation consisting of over 13,500 large and small islands stretching over 3,200 miles east to west and over 1,100 miles north and south. Its geographical expanse, therefore, is almost equal to that of the continental United States. Its principal islands are Java, Sumatra, Sulawesi, Borneo (Kalimantan is the portion belonging to Indonesia), and New Guinea (Irian Jaya is the Indonesian portion). One of its well-known smaller islands is Bali.

Indonesia's population of 183 million people, three-fourths the population of the United States, makes it the fourth most heavily populated country in the world. Its people are ethnically diverse but predominantly Malay. Chinese constitute a small but economically important minority. Approximately two thirds of the population lives on the island of Java where the capital city of Jakarta is located. About three out of four Indonesians live in rural areas and about one out of two works in the agricultural sector.

Agriculture presently accounts for about one fourth of Indonesia's gross national product. Energy and mining accounts for about one fifth and manufacturing about one tenth. Construction and services account for the remainder.

During the early history of Indonesia, Malay people migrated from the Asiatic mainland, and Indian and Asian kingdoms colonized the region. Dutch, Portuguese, Indian, and Persian traders sailed its waters. Gradually the Dutch brought the area under their control as the Netherlands East Indies. The Dutch continued to rule for some three hundred years, until the Japanese occupied the country during World War II. The Dutch returned after the war but they were soon ousted by Indonesian nationalists led by Sukarno.

Sukarno's government was marked by political instability and a stumbling economy. An unsuccessful coup attempt in 1965 led to the subsequent transfer of leadership in 1967 to General Suharto. Suharto continues to lead the country, and his administration has compiled a remarkable record of economic progress and national unification.

An important factor in the unification of this vast and diverse country has been the government's promotion of five fundamental principles known as the *Pancasila*: Belief in One God, Nationalism, Humanitarianism, Representative Government, and Social Justice. The Pancasila have been used by the government at times to suppress divisive factions. There is no doubt they give Indonesians an important philosophical touchstone, not unlike the basic foundation the Declaration of Independence gives Americans.

Indonesia's economic growth surged in the late 1970s as a result of higher prices for its substantial oil and gas exports. Then, as oil prices fell in the early 1980s, the government moved to reduce dependence on exports of commodities, such as oil and gas, and to increase the production of manufactured goods and other value-added products. Many constructive deregulation and trade liberalization policies were implemented. Foreign investment was encouraged and financial systems improved. As a result of these and other initiatives, recent growth rates in the domestic economy and international trade of Indonesia have been impressive.

As a member of the Association of Southeast Asian Nations (ASEAN), Indonesia maintains close economic ties with Malaysia, Singapore, Thailand, the Philippines, and Brunei.

One of Indonesia's economic projects is its development of its Riau Island group (located south of Singapore), particularly Batam Island, in a "Growth Triangle" with Singapore and the Malaysian state of Johor. The concept aims to take advantage of low cost labor and land in the Riau group, low cost but skilled labor in Johor, and Singapore's financial and technological resources. The governments involved collaborated smoothly to promote the concept and to install infrastructure and industrial parks on Batam Island. A number of manufacturing facilities for electronics, garments, plastics, and other products are already in operation there.

Still a developing country, with a 1991 per capita income of only about $630, Indonesia is not yet a substantial market for American consumer products. However, strong markets exist in Indonesia for a wide range of products needed in its rapid industrial development. Americans are in a good position to capture a fair share of these markets. Under Suharto, Indonesia maintains close political and economic links with the United States, and Americans are well liked by the Indonesians. American exporters should view Indonesia as a source of significant long-term opportunities.

## NEAR-TERM OUTLOOK

Indonesia's economic vitality will continue, thanks to abundant resources and a stable political environment. President Suharto will be elected to a sixth five-year term in March 1993. Government policies will continue to encourage economic expansion and foreign investment.

Government expenditures on improved infrastructure, together with rapid expansion of the manufacturing sector, will promote inflation in the short term despite tight money policies. Nonetheless, inflation will be held below eight percent in 1993.

The economy is forecast to grow by six percent in 1993, paced by manufacturing growth of twelve percent. Service industry growth will exceed seven percent. Indonesia's trade liberalization efforts will be accelerated. Tariffs will be reduced on hundreds of products, and other trade barriers will be relaxed. Imports will expand by eleven percent in 1993. Exports are expected to rise fifteen percent.

## LANGUAGE

There are about 365 separate languages and dialects spoken in Indonesia, but Bahasa Indonesia, a Malay-based language, is the official language and is understood by most Indonesians. English is spoken at senior levels of business and government and by many Indonesians who are in frequent contact with international visitors.

Americans who spend some time in Indonesia are strongly advised to learn as much Bahasa Indonesia as possible. It is fundamentally a trading language, and its alphabet and sounds are familiar to people who speak English. It is one of the easier languages to learn.

**RELIGION**

Islam is the principal religion of Indonesia; Muslims constitute about 85 percent of the population. Other prominent religions are Christianity (about six percent), Buddhism (about two percent), and Hinduism (about one percent).

**VITAL ECONOMIC STATISTICS (1991 Estimates)**

| | |
|---|---|
| Population: | 183 million |
| Gross Domestic Product | US$ 111 billion |
| Income Per Capita | US$ 631 |
| Annual Growth Rate | 6 percent |
| Total Imports | US$ 25.5 billion |
| Total Exports | US$ 29.3 billion |
| U.S. Share of Manufactured Imports | 10.5 percent |
| U.S. Share of Total Exports | 12.5 percent |

**Top Five Imports From U.S.**

Industrial chemicals
Plastic materials and resins
Ships, boats, and floating structures
Civil engineering and contractors' equipment
Computers and peripherals

**Top Five Exports To U.S.**

Crude oil and petroleum products
Garments and apparel
Plywood and other wood products
Footwear products
Furniture and parts

**Top Three Foreign Investors**

Japan
Hong Kong
U.S.

**Top Three Trading Partners**

Japan
U.S.
Germany

**BEST EXPORT OPPORTUNITIES FOR AMERICAN FIRMS***

**Industrial Chemicals**

Unsaturated ethylene, benzene and toluene, P-xylene, styrene, vinyl chloride, ethylene glycol, phenol and its salts, vinyl acetate, and others

**Iron and Steel**

Slabs, rectangular blooms, flat rolled products, coils

**Plastic Materials and Resins**

Polyethylene, polyvinyl chloride, other polyethers, polypropylene, polyamides, polyvinyl alcohols

**Textile Machinery and Equipment**

Carding machines, textile spinning machines, textile doubling/twisting machines, textile winding or reeling machines, weaving and knitting machines, footwear machines

---

* U.S. Department of Commerce 1992 Rankings

| | |
|---|---|
| **Automotive Parts and Service Equipment** | Brakes, gear boxes, drive axles, steering wheels and columns, suspension shock absorbers, clutches |
| **Electric Power Systems** | Water tube boilers, vapor generating boilers, super heated water boilers, turbines for marine propulsion, generating sets with compression ignition, gas turbines, parts |
| **Construction Equipment** | Boring and sinking machinery, buckets, shovels, bulldozers, hydraulic excavators, off-road trucks |
| **Pumps, Valves, and Compressors** | Concrete pumps, centrifugal pumps, compressors, parts |
| **Commercial Vessels and Equipment** | Floating or submersible drilling or production platforms, fishing vessels, barges, cable ships, scientific research vessels |
| **Telecommunications Equipment** | Switching apparatus, transmission and reception apparatus, radar apparatus, parts |
| **Oil and Gas Field Machinery and Services** | Geophysical and geological instruments, rotary drilling surface and subsurface equipment, well completion and production equipment, pipeline equipment, workover rigs |
| **Non-Ferrous Metals** | Unwrought aluminum, cathodes, foil, unwrought zinc, unwrought refined lead, copper tubes and pipes |
| **Pulp and Paper Machinery** | Machinery for making pulp of fibrous cellulosic material, paper or paperboard, parts, offset printing machines, other printing machines |
| **Machine Tools and Metalworking Equipment** | Machine tools operated by lasers or other beam processes, numerically controlled lathes, drilling and boring machines, bending and folding machines, hydraulic presses, casting machines |
| **Yarn** | Cotton yarns, nylon and polyester yarns, cellulose acetate yarn, multiple yarns |
| **Materials Handling Machinery** | Forklifts, gantry and bridge cranes, elevators, lifts and skip hoists, conveyor idlers, escalators and moving walkways |
| **Aircraft and Parts** | Aircraft, propellers and rotors, engines, undercarriages, parts |
| **Process Control—Industrial** | Surveying instruments, measuring and checking equipment, gas and smoke analysis apparatus, automatic regulating and controlling equipment |
| **Forestry and Woodworking Machinery** | Sawing, milling, planing, molding machines, presses, grinding, sanding, polishing machines, bending and assembling machines, splitting, slicing and paring machines |

| | |
|---|---|
| **Computers and Peripherals** | Main frame and other computers, digital processing units, data processing machines, parts and accessories |
| **Paper and Paperboard** | Bank notes paper, industrial sack paper, cigarette paper, bleached and coated papers, wadding webs, writing paper |
| **Air-Conditioning and Refrigeration Equipment** | Refrigerating and freezing equipment, air-conditioning machines, heat exchange units, dryers, heating and cooling plants, parts |
| **Food Processing and Packaging Equipment** | Machinery for cleaning and sorting seed, for extraction and preparation of fats and oils, for preparation of fruits, nuts and vegetables, packaging machines, parts |
| **Architectural, Construction, and Engineering Services** | Engineering studies and designs, construction services and supervision for major projects |
| **Consumer Electronics** | TV sets, radios, speakers and amplifiers, washing machines, home electric appliances, components and parts |
| **Plastics Production Machinery** | Injection-molding machines, extruders, flow-molding machines, other machines for working rubber or plastics |
| **Drugs and Pharmaceuticals** | Vaccines, contraceptive preparations, penicillins, tetracyclines, other antibiotics chloramphenicol and derivatives |
| **Photographic Equipment and Supplies** | Camera parts and accessories, developing equipment, instruments for laboratories, instruments for surveying |
| **Mining Equipment** | Conveyors, bulldozers, hydraulic excavators, mechanical shovels, boring and sinking machinery, off-road trucks, parts |
| **Building Products** | Paints, varnishes, bricks, blocks, tiles, refractory items, floor tiles, door locks |

## BUSINESS PRACTICES

### Meetings

Business is conducted rather informally in Indonesia. Although appointments can be arranged on short notice, persons traveling to Indonesia from overseas should make appointments well in advance for those they need to see.

It is helpful to take an Indonesian colleague with you to meetings. Indonesian culture has a long tradition of friends serving as facilitators during discussion of important issues. When appropriate, your colleague can assume the role of facilitator, assisting you in bringing about a smooth and successful conclusion to your meeting.

Punctuality is not as important as it is elsewhere in Asia. Do not be surprised or show annoyance if Indonesians are late to a meeting. However, you should not be the one to be late. And allow plenty of time to conclude your business. Meetings tend to be long, slow, and frustrating for Americans, but attempting to accelerate the process tends to be counterproductive.

**Business Hours**   Most business offices are open five days a week, Monday through Friday, from 8 a.m. to 5 p.m. Government offices and some business offices are open on Saturday from 8 a.m. to 1 p.m. A lunch hour is normally taken on weekdays at noon or 12:30 p.m.

**Greetings**   In Indonesia, greetings are made with warmth but not gusto. A nod of the head and an exchange of pleasantries is the custom. Politeness is especially important. It is not customary to bow. Indonesians normally shake hands only upon first meeting or on leaving for or returning from a trip, although in business circles it has now become a common practice for men and women. One shakes hands lightly, not with a firm grip.

**Business Cards**   Cards are always exchanged on first meeting. They need not be printed in Bahasa Indonesia on one side. Flashy cards are admired in Indonesia. Your educational degrees — particularly advanced degrees — can be added to your name as they too are admired and respected in Indonesia.

**Names and Titles**   There is great diversity of customs and practices when it comes to Indonesian names and titles. Some Indonesians have only one name and no family name. For example, Suharto is President Suharto's only name. When a family name is used, it can either appear first or last depending upon one's ethnic group and personal preference.

Indonesians are normally addressed with an honorific, as in "Bapak Hasan." Government officials and professional people are usually addressed with a title, as in "Minister Noor" or "Engineer Sjahrir." If there is no title, older persons and superiors are normally addressed with the honorific "Bapak" or "Pak" (the word for father) or "Ibu" (the word for mother), as in "Bapak Noor" or "Ibu Sjahrir."

The most prudent advice for Americans is to ask an Indonesian colleague how to address a certain person, or to ask the person directly. And when in doubt, simply use "Mr.," "Mrs.," or "Miss." "Ms." should not be used. If you are unsure of a woman's marital status, use "Mrs."

**Clothing**   Dress for warm weather. Indonesia lies just south of the equator, and it is warm and humid. For men, a white shirt and tie are normal, except for first meetings and meetings with government officials, when a jacket should be worn. A dress or skirt and blouse is normal for women.

Long sleeved, open neck, batik shirts are appropriate for men in the evening and on most formal occasions. Indonesian men and women often wear colorful cotton batik clothing in the evening and on informal occasions. Most Americans enjoy buying and wearing batik during their visits to Indonesia.

**Gifts and Entertainment**   Gifts are important but need not be elaborate. Gifts associated with your organization or your part of the United States are the most successful.

Business entertaining at hotels and restaurants is common, but Indonesians rarely do business entertaining in their homes. If you are invited to dinner at an Indonesian home, it is appropriate to take the hostess a gift, such as candy, cookies, or flowers (but not wine or liquor if the family is Muslim). Americans who are entertained during their visit should reciprocate before returning home. An Indonesian colleague, or their hotel, can help with the arrangements.

**Conversation**

Family-related topics are the most interesting to Indonesians. You can expect to be asked a number of personal questions. You can, in turn, ask similar questions, but it is best not to ask questions about an Indonesian's income or material circumstances. American and Indonesian lifestyles, and the beauty and economic progress of Indonesia, are also good topics of conversation. Indonesian political issues are sensitive and should be avoided, but Americans may freely discuss political events in the United States.

**Hotels**

Business travelers have the choice of several modern hotels in Jakarta but elsewhere the choice is more limited. Service and dining generally are excellent throughout Indonesia. Make your hotel reservations in advance as you normally would do.

**Exercise**

The Indonesian heat might inhibit one's good intentions when it comes to the exercise department. However, jogging or walking in the early morning or evening is enjoyable. Also, some hotels and a number of private clubs (to which your Indonesian colleagues might belong) have swimming pools and other exercise facilities. Standard athletic wear is acceptable attire for men and women.

**Transportation and Communications**

Taxis are the best means of transportation in the cities. Taxis normally have meters, and you should make sure that the meter is started when the ride begins. If transportation is needed outside the cities or for several destinations, you should consider hiring a car and driver for the day. This can be arranged easily by your hotel.

Telecommunications are excellent in hotels and business offices in Jakarta. Fax machines are in wide use there and international courier services are available. Elsewhere in Indonesia the facilities are not as satisfactory.

**Special Considerations**

Indonesians are sensitive to gestures and body contact. Americans should not stand with hands on hips (this is rudely aggressive) or point at someone with a finger (instead, one should indicate with a wave of the hand). One should not touch another person's head. Also, one should not touch someone or take food with the left hand; this is the "unclean" hand, used at the toilet.

While there is little threat of physical danger in Indonesia, thieves and pickpockets are prevalent in some parts of Indonesian cities and on public conveyances. Therefore, you should take the usual precautions to guard your personal belongings: lock the windows of your room when going out, place special valuables in a hotel safe, and wear a money belt if walking in crowded areas.

**ENTRY REQUIREMENTS**

Americans on business will need a passport valid for at least six months, a visa, sufficient funds for the stay, and a ticket and documents for onward passage.

**MONEY**

The unit of currency is the rupiah (Rp.). Cash is easily obtained at banks and hotels. Major credit cards are widely accepted throughout Indonesia. International travelers checks are accepted in hotels but often not in shops.

One U.S. dollar is equal to about 2,000 rupiahs.

**TIPPING**

Tipping on a modest scale is common in Indonesian cities, but there is no tipping elsewhere. In restaurants, check to see if a service charge has been added. If not, a small tip for good service may be appropriate, depending on the restaurant. A tip of ten percent would be considered very generous. Tip 100 rupiahs to attendants and for small services, 200 rupiahs to taxi drivers (regardless of the length of the ride), and up to 300 rupiahs per bag to porters. Special services, such as those of a driver, should be acknowledged more generously and with a small gift such as an American souvenir.

For tipping, it is difficult to deal with change of less than 100 rupiahs (about five cents in U.S. currency). Therefore, tips are usually rounded up to the next multiple of five, for example, to Rp. 500, Rp. 1,000, Rp. 1,500.

**MAJOR HOLIDAYS**

| | |
|---|---|
| New Year's Day | January 1 |
| Ascension Day | January* |
| Lailat Al-Mi'raj | January/February* |
| Good Friday | Friday before Easter |
| Easter | March/April* |
| Lebaran | March/April (two days)* |
| Waisak | May* |
| Idul Adha | July* |
| First Muharan | July* |
| Independence Day | August 17 |
| Maulud of Prophet Muhammad | October* |
| Christmas Day | December 25 |

**USEFUL PHRASES**

| English | Bahasa Indonesia | Phonetic Pronunciation |
|---|---|---|
| Welcome | Selamat datang | Suh-lah-maht da-tahng |
| Good morning | Selamat pagi | Suh-lah-maht pah-gee |
| Good afternoon | Selamat sore | Suh-lah-maht so-ray |
| Good evening | Selamat malam | Suh-lah-maht mah-lahm |
| Good night | Selamat tidur | Suh-lah-maht tee-duhr |
| Good-bye (to guest) | Selamat djalan | Suh-lah-maht jah-lahn |
| Good-bye (to host) | Selamat tinggal | Suh-lah-maht teen-gahl |
| Yes | Ya | Yah |
| No | Tidak | Tee-dahk |
| Please | Silakan | See-lah-kahn |
| Come in | Silakan masuk | See-lah-kahn mah-sook |
| How much? | Barapa harganya? | Bar-ah-pah har-gahn-yah? |
| Thank you | Terima kasih | Teh-ree-mah cah-see |
| You're welcome | Kembali | kem-bah-lee |
| Cheers | Selamat | Suh-lah-maht |
| I don't understand | Saya tidak mengerti | Sah-ya tee-dahk men-gehr-tee |

---

\* Date varies

In pronouncing Bahasa Indonesia, place the accent on the next-to-last syllable of each word. For example, silakan masuk (come in) is pronounced see-LAH-kahn MAH-sook.

## USEFUL INDONESIAN CONTACTS

National Development Information Office
Wisma Antara
Jalan Medan Medeka Selatan 17
Jakarta 10110, Indonesia
TELEPHONE: 62*/21/384-7412
FAX: 62-21/384-7603

Indonesian Chambers of Commerce and Industry
Chandra Boulevard
Jalan M. H. Thamrin 20
Jakarta, Indonesia
TELEPHONE: 62-21/310-5683
FAX: 62-21/350-442

United States Embassy
Commercial Section
Jalan Medan Medeka Selatan 5
Jakarta, Indonesia
TELEPHONE: 62-21/360-360
FAX: 62-21/360-644

American Chamber of Commerce
P.O. Box 3060
Landmark Centre
Jalan Jenderal Sudirman Kav 70A
Jakarta, Indonesia
TELEPHONE: 62-21/578-0658
FAX: 62-21/571-0656

Importers' Association of Indonesia
P.O. Box 2244/JKT
Jalan E Pintu Timur Arena PRJ
Jakarta, Indonesia
TELEPHONE: 62-21/377-008
FAX: 62-21/324-422

---

\* Indonesia's country code

# COUNTRY PROFILE: JAPAN

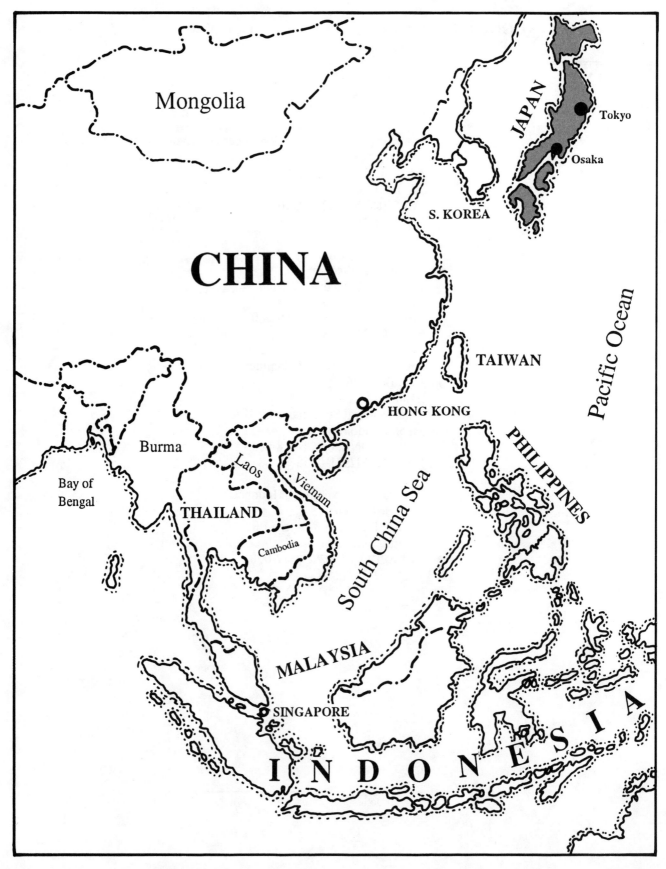

## LIGHTING THE WAY IN JAPAN

"In today's leading edge technologies, the most important customers and competitors are likely to be in Japan," says Don Spero, President of Fusion Systems Corporation of Rockville, Maryland.

Spero is one of five scientists and engineers who started Fusion in the early 1970s with an innovative technology for producing microwave-powered ultraviolet curing lamps. Fusion's super high intensity lamps dry a wide range of inks, coatings, and adhesives in industrial applications, from the printing on a can of beer to coatings on silicon chips. Its lamps are integrated with machinery in many industries including the automotive, semiconductor, and graphic arts industries.

Today Fusion employs 325 people and occupies 115,000 square feet of space in Rockville, where it does all of its manufacturing. The company offers dramatic proof that a small, entrepreneurial, private firm can succeed in a global marketplace. With annual sales of about $40 million, Fusion has customers in 30 countries and exports 46 percent of its production.

Japan is Fusion's largest overseas market, representing 29 percent of its total sales. In 1986, because of the growing importance of its Japanese markets, Fusion established a wholly owned subsidiary in country to provide greatly improved sales and service as well as local engineering and process support. Today Fusion has fifteen employees in Japan, only one of whom is an American. The operation is headed by a Japanese, Teruo Orikasa, the first employee of Fusion Japan.

"Japan is key to us not only because it is the home of our most important customers, competitors, and suppliers," says Spero, "but also because it has a leading position in many key industries to which we sell our production equipment." He adds, "Certainly Japan offers difficult challenges — barriers of language, culture, and differing expectations, to name just a few. But challenges and opportunities typically present themselves as a package, and that is the case here. Japan offers greater challenges but also greater opportunities."

Fusion's success in Japan has not been achieved easily. Fusion first entered the Japanese market in 1975, when the company's total revenues were less than $1 million. "Our sales in Japan were insignificant for the first five years," says Spero. "In these early years we worked hard to establish customer relationships and get a realistic feel for how business is done in Japan. We learned the importance of modifying our products to meet the unique requirements of Japanese customers."

Protection of its technology has been a special problem for Fusion in Japan. Despite having established patents for its products in the country, Fusion discovered in 1986 that Mitsubishi Electric Company had filed patents for innumerable modifications of basic Fusion technology. This is a tactic called "patent flooding," aimed at forcing Fusion to cross-license its core technology. But Spero is upbeat about the problem. "Our fundamental strategy," he says, "is simply to stay ahead in innovation and to cultivate and maintain valued customer relationships in Japan."

"We need to be in Japan," says Spero. "If we can succeed there, we'll be positioned to succeed anywhere."

## JAPAN: ECONOMIC BACKGROUND

When United States trade representatives complained to Japanese officials in recent years about Japanese trade barriers, the Japanese often responded, "Americans must try harder."

The Japanese are tough customers. They are tough on their suppliers, their competitors, their partners and associates ... and they are tough on themselves. At the same time, the Japanese are great customers and colleagues, and once they are sold or committed, they are loyal and steadfast.

Americans who wish to sell to the Japanese must indeed try hard. They must offer products and services that meet high standards of quality and that appeal to the unique tastes and needs of the Japanese. If they succeed, the rewards are immense because the Japanese have deep pockets and expanding appetites.

After the United States, Japan's economy is now the second largest in the world. For an island nation having limited natural resources, a small fraction (4%) of the land area of the United States, and less than one half the population of the United States, Japan's economic strength and achievements are remarkable.

Following World War II, and with substantial assistance from the United States, Japan founded its economic revival on an increasingly advanced and innovative manufacturing base. Its growth strategies, at first export-driven, are now concentrating in large part on domestic economic growth and on investment outside Japan.

On the domestic side, Japan is investing heavily in infrastructure. Facilities and systems that were neglected in Japan's rush to dominate international commercial markets are now receiving attention. Huge sums are to be spent on airports, bridges, roads, port development projects, telecommunications systems, resorts, retirement communities, medical centers, and educational institutions. Also, finally reacting to prodding from the United States and other nations, Japan is gradually lowering trade barriers and raising domestic consumer demand.

To spur consumer demand, Japan is consciously easing up on its heavy work ethic. Leaders in government and industry are no longer exhorting workers to sacrifice their personal lives for the nation's economic progress. Quite the opposite, in fact. One such leader, Akio Morita, chairman of Sony Corporation, recently challenged Japanese companies to abandon practices that focus on the selfish pursuit of economic interests and to share more of their bounty with employees and shareholders.

On the international side, Japan is emphasizing direct foreign investment, investing in production facilities in countries outside Japan, and establishing strong economic ties with those countries. While its investments span the globe, its principal focus for a number of years has been Asia, especially countries in Southeast Asia. Two 1990 surveys of Japanese firms with investment plans overseas (one by Japan's Export-Import Bank) showed Southeast Asia as the top priority investment site. (Thailand was the most popular site, followed by Indonesia and Malaysia.)

Such investments by Japan's private sector are backed up frequently by Japanese government aid, "official development assistance," that must be used by host countries in ways that support the investments. Recently Japan has directed more of its foreign aid toward such support and away from general infrastructure projects like dams and bridges.

These developments have great significance for American exporters. As a result of changes in their domestic economic policy, the Japanese are beginning to work fewer hours, save less, and spend more. As a result of Japan's direct foreign investment and its aid policies, Japan is financing growing markets throughout the region and the world. The opportunities for American exporters in these circumstances are substantial.

American firms that succeed in Japan normally give credit for their accomplishments to a willingness to adapt their products and services to the market, their agreeing to "conform to the system" rather than try to change it, and their ability to sustain early setbacks. Because Japanese society is so different from American society, despite the long and close association between the two countries in the years since World War II, market knowledge and cultural understanding are especially important.

The cultural contrasts between Americans and Japanese are many, due in large part to historical and geographic differences. One important difference is that the United States was settled in recent centuries by migrants from a wide variety of national and ethnic backgrounds, and the United States pins its national identity on this open mixture. Japan, on the other hand, was settled centuries earlier by Asiatic migrants who coalesced into a largely homogeneous population. Another difference is that Americans have the luxury of wide open spaces and abundant resources; they are accustomed to spreading out and being somewhat carefree. The Japanese, however, are confined to limited space and have to conserve their few resources with care.

These and many other factors result in Japanese attitudes that are resistive to things that are new or different and to products and services that fail to measure up to exacting standards of quality.

Asian cultural factors, discussed in Chapter 3, are especially applicable to Japan. Collectivist attitudes and traditions are strong. The group-orientation of Japanese, for example, accounts in part for the difficulties Americans often face in breaking into markets served by Japanese competitors or in establishing joint ventures and other business relationships with Japanese firms. Japanese firms tend to establish exclusive networks with other Japanese firms, even overseas. Most of these networks are informal. However, there are large groupings of companies, called *keiretsu,* like Mitsubishi and Sumitomo, in which there are crossholdings of large blocks of each others' stock. (*Keiretsu* means linkage in Japanese.)

Nonetheless, relations between Americans and the Japanese are characterized by warmth and mutual respect. Cultural understanding is growing. Frictions due to the trade imbalance between the two countries are being ameliorated by an open discussion of problems. Through candid and sometimes emotional exchanges, the critical issues have been brought to the attention of wide audiences in each country. In the United States, people are now asking "How come we aren't exporting right hand drive cars to Japan?" In Japan, where prices are inflated by inefficient distribution systems and where workers still subsidize economic growth with long hours and low pay, people are beginning to ask, "If we're so rich, how come we don't live better?"

As trade relations between the two countries improve, opportunities for American exporters in Japan will continue to expand. The rewards are there for Americans who will "try hard."

**NEAR-TERM OUTLOOK**

In 1993, Japan's economy will regain some of the momentum it lost as a result of the 1990-1992 world economic slowdown and the near-collapse in 1992 of some of its financial institutions (many Japanese banks and other lenders had over-committed to stock market and real estate speculators.) Industrial production will rise by three percent in 1993, and inflation should remain below three percent.

Although household incomes will not rise appreciably in the short term, Japanese appetites for upscale consumer goods and leisure activities, such as vacations, travel, golf, and pleasure boating, will rise. Also, the government will continue to push its ambitious domestic spending programs for improved housing, transportation, public parks, environmental protection, and welfare for the elderly. However, industrial companies are apt to cut back on capital investment plans as a result of lenders' new-found conservatism.

Imports will rise by seven percent and exports by six percent in 1993. Modest progress should be made in the reduction of trade barriers.

**LANGUAGE**

A standard dialect of Japanese is understood throughout Japan, and the written language, in addition to ideographic (kanji) characters, is in standardized script.

Unfortunately—for Americans and other foreign businessmen—Japan has few street signs in roman letters, and street addresses are complicated. Accordingly, when you leave your hotel, it is a good idea to carry with you the addresses of your appointments written in Japanese in order to ask directions or give your destination.

Fortunately, many Japanese (especially younger Japanese) understand English. English is the most frequently taught foreign language in Japanese schools. Americans should be aware, however, that the Japanese tend to read English better than they understand spoken English.

**RELIGION**

Buddhism and Shintoism are the principal religions of Japan. Less than one percent of the population is Christian.

**VITAL ECONOMIC STATISTICS (1991 Estimates)**

| | |
|---|---|
| Population: | 124 million |
| Gross Domestic Product | US$ 3.4 trillion |
| Income Per Capita | US$ 27,200 |
| Annual Growth Rate | 3.5 percent |
| Total Imports | US$ 243.6 billion |
| Total Exports | US$ 305.4 billion |
| U.S. Share of Manufactured Imports | 23.2 percent |
| U.S. Share of Total Exports | 29.0 percent |

**Top Five Imports From U.S.**

Automatic data processing machines and office equipment
Wood, rough or roughly squared
Aircraft, spacecraft, and associated equipment
Fish and seafood products
Semiconductors and other electronic products

| | |
|---|---|
| **Top Five Exports To U.S.** | Passenger cars, buses and trucks, chassis<br>Automatic data processing machines and office equipment<br>Parts and accessories of motor vehicles<br>Scientific optical equipment<br>Semiconductors and other electronic components |
| **Top Three Foreign Investors** | U.S.<br>Switzerland<br>Netherlands |
| **Top Three Trading Partners** | U.S.<br>Germany<br>South Korea |

## BEST EXPORT OPPORTUNITIES FOR AMERICAN FIRMS*

| | |
|---|---|
| **Drugs and Pharmaceuticals** | In-vitro diagnostic test reagents, home tests |
| **Telecommunications Services** | Cordless telephone licensing, Japan-wide services |
| **Marine Fisheries Products (Seafood)** | Fresh and frozen salmon, frozen crab, frozen mackerel |
| **Biotechnology Products** | Pharmaceuticals, chemicals |
| **Medical Equipment and Supplies** | Diagnostic imaging equipment, implantable devices |
| **Industrial Chemicals** | Specialty chemicals |
| **Aircraft and Parts** | Military aircraft, civil aviation aircraft |
| **Architectural, Construction, and Engineering Services** | Private projects, resorts in western Japan, Sports Island, Kyoto Station Building, Synchrotron projects |
| **Sporting Goods** | Golf equipment, outdoor equipment, pleasure boats, fitness equipment |
| **Computer Software and Services** | PC software, baseline software for mainframes |
| **Building Products** | Wooden windows, wooden flooring |
| **Laboratory Scientific Instruments** | Electric test and measurement instruments, analytical instrumentation |
| **Computers and Peripherals** | Workstations, supercomputers |
| **Plastic Materials and Resins** | Engineering plastics |

---

* U.S. Department of Commerce 1992 Rankings

| | |
|---|---|
| **Automotive Parts and Service Equipment** | High technology parts and equipment, turbochargers, catalytic converters, shock absorbers, emission control devices, air bags products |
| **Films/Videos** | Film distribution, rental videos, home videos |
| **Jewelry** | Diamonds, costume jewelry |
| **Telecommunications Equipment** | Communications satellites, launch services, cellular infrastructure equipment, switching and control units |
| **Apparel** | Ladies' wear, men's wear |
| **Household Consumer Goods** | Decorative interior products, lighting equipment |
| **Machine Tools and Metalworking Equipment** | Metal cutting machine tools, grinding machines, gear cutting machines |
| **Process Control—Industrial** | Process analyzers |
| **CAD/CAM/CAE/CIM** | (Computer Assisted Design/Manufacturing/Engineering; Computer Integrated Manufacturing) PC and EWS based CAD/CAM/CAE |
| **Foods—Processed** | Health food and vitamins |
| **Paper and Paperboard** | Hospital sanitary products, value-added paper products |
| **Electronic Components** | Gallium arsenic integrated circuits, liquid crystal display drivers |
| **Electronics Industry Production and Test Equipment** | Semiconductor production and test equipment, flat panel display production and test equipment |
| **Giftware** | Home accessories, handicrafts |
| **Veterinary Equipment and Supplies** | Pet food |
| **Automobiles and Light Trucks and Vans** | Subcompact/compact passenger cars |
| **Advanced Ceramics** | Electromagnetic components, chemical and medical components |
| **Pollution Control Equipment** | Toxic waste removal and decontamination equipment, recovery or recycling equipment and systems, recycling and disposal equipment for waste plastics |
| **Cosmetics** | Make-up preparations, hair care preparations |

| | |
|---|---|
| **Health Care Services** | Hospital support, home care services |
| **Furniture** | Furniture for city and resort hotels, systems furniture for offices |
| **Air-Conditioning and Refrigeration Equipment** | Window type air conditioners, freezers and ice-making machines, refrigerating machines |
| **Textile Products** | Curtains, carpets |
| **Security Equipment** | Burglar sensor systems, advanced access control systems |
| **Printing and Graphic Arts Equipment** | Offset printing machinery, platemaking machinery and equipment |
| **Coal** | Industrial uses |

## BUSINESS PRACTICES

**Meetings**

Not only must business appointments be made well in advance, it is very important that you be properly introduced by someone who knows you and is known to the Japanese person or firm you wish to meet. If you do not have a relationship with an organization or individual who can perform this service, the Japan External Trade Organization (JETRO) can make introductions for you.

Thorough preparations should be made even for informal meetings. For the best and most persuasive effect, presentation materials should be translated into Japanese. If a meeting is expected to include discussions or negotiations, an agenda and discussion materials should be submitted to the Japanese side in advance.

Punctuality is important, as are politeness and decorum. Once underway, meetings can be lengthy—if the subject matter is detailed and important. American businessmen may need to "invest" in many days of meetings and repeated visits to Japan before a business transaction is concluded.

**Business Hours**

Offices are open five days a week, Monday through Friday, 9 a.m. to 5 p.m., with an hour for lunch normally taken at noon. Workers often are at their desks well into the evenings and on Saturday mornings, but the practice of (virtually required) long hours is gradually beginning to abate.

**Greetings**

Japanese greet each other with a bow, the lower the bow the more respectful the greeting. They do not normally shake hands, but in business circles they do so with Americans and other Westerners. Americans normally can combine a bow and a handshake when meeting a Japanese, with the bow coming first. One shakes hands lightly, not firmly.

**Business Cards**

Business cards are very important and are always exchanged on first meeting. They are presented with a degree of ceremony, with the print facing the person to whom presented, and preferably with both hands, never in an offhand manner. When receiving a card from a Japanese, one should study it for a moment and give a nod of acknowledgment.

Your business cards should be printed in Japanese script on one side.

Be certain that your title is included and fully reflects your responsibilities. Also, consult a native Japanese who knows English to be sure that the translation is correct. Cards should be carried where they are easily accessible and can be neatly maintained, not stuffed where they become crumpled or soiled.

**Names and Titles**

Titles are not used in addressing people in Japan. Instead, people are addressed by their family names, which appear last when written, and the suffix "-san" is added to the end of the name, as in "Mori-san." This is true for both men and women. First names are never used except between very close friends.

Americans will be tempted to address their Japanese friends by their first names, but they should not do so. Instead, always use the "-san" suffix or "Mr.," "Dr.," "Ms.," or "Mrs.," as appropriate. The observance of this Japanese custom will be appreciated more than the gesture of friendship.

The first names of Japanese women, incidentally, often end in "ko," as in Michiko and Fukiko. This is a familiar usage, similar to the ending "ie" in names of American women like "Jackie." By itself, "ko" means child in Japanese.

**Clothing**

Men and women should dress conservatively in Japan. For men, suits and ties of muted or dark colors. For women, suits or skirts and blouses, or conservative dresses. On informal occasions, sports jackets and open-neck shirts are appropriate for men. Shorts are not appropriate for men or women except when engaged in sports or exercise.

**Gifts and Entertainment**

Gift-giving is very important in Japan. Gifts should be thoughtful but not lavish. Ones associated with your organization or your part of the United States are especially appropriate. As the Japanese are status-conscious, brand name gifts are particularly popular.

Gifts should not be too personal in nature (such as a cologne), but items for personal use (such as pens or cassette tapes) are fine. So are T-shirts for the children of a Japanese family.

Gifts should be neatly wrapped in pastel-colored paper without ribbons or bows. Your hotel can do the wrapping, if you wish. Gifts are presented and received with both hands. If you receive a gift, it should not be opened in the presence of the giver unless the giver strongly insists. The best timing for gift-giving is early in a first meeting or toward the end of a final meeting.

Business entertaining is common, normally at dinner or for cocktails after business hours. Because the Japanese believe alcohol improves relations, drinking can be heavy on these occasions. Americans who do not wish to drink heavily should abstain completely "on doctor's orders" (an acceptable excuse) rather than be perceived as a reluctant participant.

The Japanese normally entertain in restaurants, bars, and hotels. They seldom entertain in their homes (an invitation to the home of a Japanese businessman with whom you are doing or plan to do business is considered an honor bestowed on the invitee). Dining establishments are everywhere. In fact, there are more restaurants per capita in Japan than anywhere else in the world.

Americans should present a gift to a Japanese host or hostess when entertained, especially if there may not be an opportunity for reciprocal hospitality. Normally the Japanese do not expect that visitors will entertain in Japan unless in connection with a series of meetings.

Americans should send a thank-you note or letter to a Japanese host after being entertained. Also, the next time they see the host (whether on the following day or months later), they should say how much they enjoyed the occasion.

**Conversation**

The Japanese are patriotic people and very proud of their country. Accordingly, Japan's unique customs, economic success, and natural beauty are good topics of conversation. The Japanese also are self-conscious as a people and are always interested in how Americans and others perceive them, so long as criticism is not implied. Although they are also highly family-oriented and will enjoy hearing about your family, they are private people and are not comfortable in talking at length about their own families.

Golf is always a good topic of conversation in Japan. So is American baseball. The Japanese are avid sports fans. Among younger Japanese, American movies are fodder for good conversation. Politics and religion are topics that are best avoided.

**Hotels**

Despite the greater expense, American business people should plan to stay in one of the better hotels. In the opinion of the status-conscious Japanese, one's hotel reflects one's importance and good taste. Americans also will find many more conveniences in these hotels, including a greater number of English-speaking staff.

Make hotel reservations well in advance, especially in Tokyo and Osaka. To be sure that you will be able to find your way back to your hotel, carry one of the hotel's cards or matchbooks with its address written in Japanese to show to a taxi driver, policeman, or pedestrian.

**Exercise**

Conditions in many Japanese cities are not conducive to exercise, although some jogging and walking is feasible and the larger hotels have exercise facilities. Probably the best activity is walking the side streets near your hotel. This not only provides a practical and accessible form of exercise, it gives you an opportunity to learn much about how the Japanese live and work. The Tokyo subway system affords plenty of stair climbing and walking exercise in making connections. Virtually all neighborhoods are safe, but there is little protection against getting lost. When you explore in this way, always carry a good map of the area.

**Transportation and Communications**

Although this may seem inconsistent on the part of the Japanese, Americans who stay in the best hotels of Tokyo do not lose face by riding the subway. Because Tokyo's streets are so crowded, the subway often is the most efficient means of transportation. And the Japanese will be impressed with the navigational skills of Americans who master the system.

Otherwise, taxis are the best transportation in Japan's cities. The taxis have meters, and the driver opens the passenger doors with controls from the driver's seat. Avoid all forms of transportation during rush hours, if you can. Also, night owls need to keep in mind that Japan's transportation systems shut down early. Even a taxi in Tokyo is hard to find after midnight.

In traveling outside the cities, Japan's railways and commuter trains provide excellent transportation.

Communications—telephones with international direct dialing, fax machines, the postal service, courier and messenger services—are all excellent and readily available in Japanese cities. Automatic fax machines are even available in the 24-hour convenience stores that are found throughout Japan's cities.

**Special Considerations**

Businesses relating to leisure (for example, travel, entertainment, education, clothing, sporting goods) are developing rapidly in Japan.

The Japanese are especially motivated by product quality and acceptance. Hence, American goods and services with established reputations and brand names, known for quality and accepted widely by others—especially other Japanese—sell easily. For example, L. L. Bean currently is enjoying substantial success in Japan.

The Japanese also have a strong urge to conform to group behavior. Some call this a herding instinct (observe the behavior of a group of Japanese tourists, obviously traveling together, in an international airport and note the sameness of the gifts they are bringing home). One consequence of this phenomenon is that sales can skyrocket when something "catches on" in Japan.

In matters of taste, however, the Japanese are beginning to express more individuality. In this regard, the range of their preferences in food and clothing has expanded significantly in recent years.

Except on subways and other crowded places where there is no alternative, the Japanese appreciate physical space and privacy. Touching and other casual body contact is not welcomed. Staring and prolonged eye contact is considered rude.

Japanese society is highly male oriented. Do not expect to see women in senior positions at Japanese firms. American business women might be annoyed to find that Japanese men often pay greater deference to their male assistants. However, Japanese men otherwise have little difficulty in dealing with American business women as equals.

Serious business is done on the golf course in Japan, and an invitation to play is an indication that the Japanese host values highly an existing or potential relationship with a guest. Americans who are invited to play golf have an excellent opportunity to strengthen their business ties with their hosts.

**ENTRY REQUIREMENTS**

Americans need their passports, sufficient funds for the stay, and tickets and documents for onward travel. Visas are required for visits of more than 90 days.

**MONEY**

The unit of currency in Japan is the yen (¥). Cash is easily obtained at banks and hotels. Except in small establishments, major credit cards and international travelers checks are widely accepted throughout Japan.

One U.S. dollar is equal to about ¥125.

**TIPPING**

Essentially there is no tipping in Japan. Except for porters at airports or train stations, who expect to receive a flat ¥200, the Japanese are offended by the gesture. An attempt to tip a taxi driver, for example, will probably be refused with some annoyance. However, when your visit is concluded, it is appropriate to reward the especially attentive services of a maid or other hotel staff member with something like ¥1,000 in an envelope (not openly handed to the person). Alternatively, a small gift such as an American souvenir is also appropriate in such circumstances. In most restaurants, a 10% or 15% service charge will be added to your bill.

**MAJOR HOLIDAYS**

| | |
|---|---|
| New Year's Day | January 1 |
| Adults' Day | January 15 |
| National Foundation Day | February 11 |
| Spring Equinox | March 21* |
| Greenery Day | April 29 |
| Constitution Day | May 3 |
| National Holiday | May 4 |
| Children's Day | May 5 |
| Respect for the Aged Day | September 15 |
| Autumnal Equinox | September 23* |
| Physical Fitness Day | October 10 |
| Cultural Day | November 3 |
| Labor Thanksgiving Day | November 23 |
| Emperor's Birthday | December 23 |

(Holidays falling on a Sunday are observed on the following day, Monday.)

Americans should be cautioned that very little business is done in Japan during the last ten days of December and first ten days of January and be aware that many Japanese are on vacation during the month of August.

**USEFUL PHRASES**

| English | Japanese | Phonetic Pronunciation |
|---|---|---|
| Hello | Hajimemashite | Hah-jee-mah-mahsh-tay |
| Good morning | Ohayo gozaimasu | O-hah-yo go-zye-mahs |
| Good afternoon | Konnichi wa | Kon-nee-chee wah |
| Good evening | Konban wa | Kon-bahn wah |
| Good-bye | Sayonara | Sigh-oh-na-ra |
| Yes | Hai | Hi |
| No | Iie | Ee-yeh |
| Please | Dozo | Doh-zo |
| How much? | Ikura desu ka? | Ee-koo-rah des kah? |
| Thank you | Arigato gozaimasu | Ah-ree-gah-toh go-zye-mahs |
| You're welcome | Do itashimashite | Doh ee-tahsh-mahsh-te |
| Cheers | Kampai | Kam-pie |
| I don't understand | Wakarimasen | Wah-kah-ree-mahs-sen |

**USEFUL JAPANESE CONTACTS**

Japan External Trade Organization (JETRO)
2-5 Toranomon 2-chome, Minato-ku
Tokyo 105, Japan
TELEPHONE: 81**/3-3582-5410
FAX: 81-3-3582-5027

---

  * Date varies
** Japan's country code

Japan External Trade Organization (JETRO)
400 North Michigan Avenue
Chicago, IL 60611
TELEPHONE: 312/527-9000
FAX: 312/670-4223

Japan External Trade Organization (JETRO)
245 Peachtree Center Avenue
Atlanta, GA 30303
TELEPHONE: 404/681-0600
FAX: 404/681-0713

Japan External Trade Organization (JETRO)
1221 McKinney, One Houston Center
Houston, TX 77010
TELEPHONE: 713/769-9595
FAX: 713/769-9210

Japan External Trade Organization (JETRO)
725 South Figueroa Street
Los Angeles, CA 90017
TELEPHONE: 213/624-8855
FAX: 213/629-8127

Japan External Trade Organization (JETRO)
1221 Avenue of the Americas
New York, NY 10020-1060
TELEPHONE: 212/997-0400
FAX: 212/997-0464

Japan External Trade Organization (JETRO)
1200 Seventeenth Street
Denver, CO 80202
TELEPHONE: 303/629-0404
FAX: 303/893-9522

Japan External Trade Organization (JETRO)
380 Post Street
San Francisco, CA 94108
TELEPHONE: 415/392-1333
FAX: 415/788-8927

Japan Foreign Trade Council
Sekai Boeki Centre Building
4-1 Hamamatsu-cho 2-chome, Minato-ku
Tokyo 105, Japan
TELEPHONE: 81-3-3435-5952
FAX: 81-3-3435-5969

Tokyo International Trade Fair Commission
7-24 Harumi 4-chome, Chuo-ku
Tokyo 100-91, Tokyo
TELEPHONE: 81-3-3531-3371
FAX: 81-3-3531-1344

United States Embassy
Commercial Section
10-1 Akasaka 1-chome, Minato-ku
Tokyo 107, Japan
TELEPHONE: 81-3-3224-5050
FAX: 81-3-3589-4235

American Chamber of Commerce
Fukide Building No. 2
1-21 Toranomon 4-chome, Minato-ku
Tokyo 105, Japan
TELEPHONE: 81-3-3433-5381
FAX: 81-3-3436-1446

The Japan Chamber of Commerce and Industry
World Trade Center Building
4-1, Hamamatsu-cho, 2-chome, Minato-ku
Tokyo 105, Japan
TELEPHONE: 81-3-3435-4785
FAX: 81-3-3578-6622

# COUNTRY PROFILE: MALAYSIA

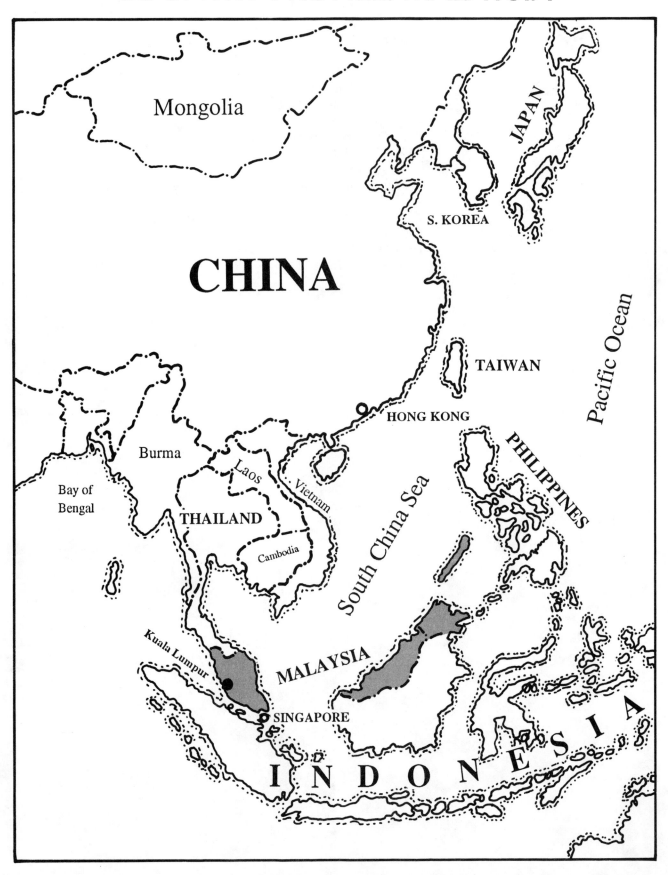

## OPENING MARKETS IN MALAYSIA

The people at Unison Corporation of Ferndale, Michigan are old Asia hands. Jack McKay and Fred McDonald, the company's founders, started developing markets in Japan in the early 1960s, soon after forming the company in 1959. From the very beginning, they made two or three trips to Asia a year.

Unison is a leading designer and manufacturer of high precision grinding systems for the automotive, off-highway, plastics, aerospace, medical, and petrochemical industries. Unison was the first grinder manufacturer to apply computerized numerical control to a grinding machine. Its machines are now used in robotic systems and in applications that grind things as small as a dental burr.

"Our company is testimony that you don't have to be a big multinational to be a player in a global market," says Gary Vasher, Unison's Director of Marketing. "We employ about 100 people, our annual sales are about $9 million, and our facilities occupy 34,000 square feet. Yet we export to more than 35 countries, mostly Europe and Asia. Exports are 40 percent of our business."

In recent years, demand for Unison's machines has been especially strong in Malaysia and other Southeast Asian countries. Sales in the region in 1991 were up approximately 20 percent over 1990. "These countries are rapidly industrializing and need Unison's state-of-the-art technology to move their manufacturing capabilities forward," says Vasher. "Grinding technology is a key segment of most manufacturing processes."

Unison's marketing strategy in Asia is two-pronged, according to Vasher. "We exhibit at machine tool trade shows throughout the region: Kuala Lumpur, Bangkok, Singapore, and Jakarta, to name a few. We also carefully select our representatives and agents and continually monitor their performance."

"Trade shows give us a chance to make new contacts and an opportunity to assess emerging market needs for our products. The shows are as important to our R & D people as they are to our marketing people," says Vasher.

Having good representatives is extremely important in Asia," adds Vasher. "Your representatives help you establish key relationships with customers there. They also solve innumerable bureaucratic problems. American exporters should not try to go into Asia alone. Language barriers are formidable, and business practices are often very different from ours."

Unison's representative in Malaysia is Nippon Machine Tool Pte., an affiliate of Siber Kikai of Japan. "We've been doing business with Siber Kikai for many years," says Vasher. "We now have a very close relationship with them. Japan is one of our most important markets in Asia, and Siber Kikai is one of the best representatives in our business in Japan and in several other Asian countries. We don't use them everywhere, however. We make an independent judgment in selecting a representative for each market we enter."

Patent infringement and "pirating" have not been problems for Unison in Asia, primarily because Unison continually improves machine quality and technology. Would-be competitors tend to develop their own technology or become a Unison customer. In one case, a Japanese company that bought a Unison manufacturing license ultimately decided to purchase equipment directly from Unison.

"We're very bullish on Asia," says Vasher. "Industrial growth is booming out there, and we think we're well positioned to participate in it."

## MALAYSIA: ECONOMIC BACKGROUND

Not unlike the legacy of a successful entrepreneur, Malaysia can be compared to a young corporation with great products, a strong balance sheet, and high ambitions. It is like a corporation moving rapidly into professional management; one in the process of defining its corporate culture, consolidating its organization, and setting long-term goals. A corporation scrambling to maintain a semblance of order in the face of rapid expansion.

Malaysia is a unique and heady mixture of diverse elements. Its 18 million people are about 56 percent Malay, 34 percent Chinese, 8 percent Indian, and 2 percent "other." Geographically, the country is divided into two parts: Peninsular Malaysia to the west, where about 85 percent of the population lives, and East Malaysia on the island of Borneo.

One of the most interesting features of Malaysia is its political system, the creation of an unusual national history. Malaysia was first settled by Asiatic people from the north. In the 15th century, the rich silk and spice trade between Europe and the Far East established the port of Malacca (situated on the west coast of Peninsular Malaysia on the Straits of Malacca) as an important trading center. First Portuguese traders, then Dutch traders, and finally British traders controlled Malacca. Gradually all of Malaysia came under British influence and control. Tin mines and rubber plantations were developed with imported Chinese and Indian labor. Trade and industry steadily grew.

Except for three years during World War II when the Japanese occupied Malaysia, the British continued to control Malaysia (which they called Malaya) until 1957. In that year, as a result of a nationalism movement born of the disruption of World War II, Malaysia declared its independence from Britain. A federation of 13 states was subsequently formed. (Singapore was originally one of 14 states of Malaysia, but it withdrew in 1965 to become an independent republic.) Nine of Malaysia's 13 states are sultanates, governed by the heirs of the sultans who once ruled them as kingdoms. The remaining four states are governed by appointed heads of state.

The Malaysian federation is an unusual constitutional monarchy in which the royalty of the nine sultanates shares power with a strong federal government and a representative parliament. Every five years the hereditary rulers of these nine states elect one of their members to serve as the King of Malaysia for the succeeding five years. The King rules on the advice of a cabinet led by a Prime Minister. In actual practice, substantial power is exercised by the Prime Minister and his cabinet ministers.

The two dominant governmental themes that emerged in Malaysia during the past two decades are social integration and economic development. Following racial disturbances in 1969, the government introduced numerous policies to enhance the status of native Malays (called Bumiputras) and promote a more equitable distribution of wealth in the country. Steps were taken to transfer some of the economic power held by Chinese Malaysians and others to Bumiputras. Significant progress has been made, eg., corporate equity in Bumiputra hands has increased from negligible amounts to about 24 percent). While these steps generated ill feelings on the part of Chinese Malaysians, economic development policies produced enough growth to satisfy the commercial appetites of all.

Malaysia has achieved some of the highest growth rates in Asia in recent years. Endowed with such substantial natural resources as oil and gas, the country long has been a major producer of tin, palm oil, natural rubber, cocoa, and hardwood. More recently, however, the combination of successful promotion of foreign investment in manufacturing and various value-added activities has resulted in a manufacturing sector that now accounts for 55 percent of all exports.

Malaysia's economic development promises to continue at a rapid clip. Under a planning program dubbed "Vision 2020," Malaysia expects to be "fully industrialized" by the year 2020. The current five year plan anticipates growth rates averaging 7.5 percent and emphasizes continued development of the manufacturing sector in addition to a substantial infrastructure build-up.

In addition, Malaysia is increasingly committed to free trade. Accordingly, trade barriers have been lowered steadily in recent years. Moreover, the government has participated in a number of free trade initiatives as an influential member of the Association of Southeast Asian Nations (ASEAN). The other ASEAN nations are Singapore, Indonesia, Thailand, the Philippines, and Brunei.

One of Malaysia's economic initiatives is participation of its state of Johor, with Indonesia and Singapore, in development of a "Growth Triangle" in Indonesia's Riau Island group (primarily on Batam Island). The Riau islands are located just south of Singapore. The concept aims to take advantage of low cost labor and land in the Riau group, low cost but skilled labor in Johor, and Singapore's financial and technological resources. The governments involved collaborated smoothly to promote the concept and to install infrastructure and industrial parks on Batam Island. A number of manufacturing facilities for electronics, garments, plastics, and other products are already in operation there.

Malaysian attitudes toward Americans and the United States are generally positive. The two countries have maintained close relations over the years and have cooperated fully on many issues, especially in the maintenance of anti-Communist policies during the Cold War years.

As a developing country, Malaysia does not yet constitute a substantial market for American consumer products. However, as per capita income grows, consumer demand is steadily increasing. Moreover, the rapid growth of Malaysia's economy is fueling strong markets for a wide range of industrial products and services as factories rise and infrastructure expands. Malaysia is a source of significant opportunity for American exporters.

## NEAR-TERM OUTLOOK

Political stability and economic growth will continue. Dr. Mahathir Mohamad will remain as Prime Minister and head of the ruling political party (United Malays National Organization, or UMNO) at least until the next general election in 1995. The economy, after catching its breath a bit with slower growth in 1992, is projected to achieve at least 8 percent growth in 1993.

With the economy at near full employment, labor shortages will be a serious problem. Wage rates and consumer spending will rise, and inflation will climb to 5 percent or higher for 1993. The government will attempt to restrain inflation with tight monetary policies but will nevertheless continue its ambitious spending programs to upgrade the country's infrastructure. Seven new gas-powered generators will boost the country's electrical generating capacity seven-fold. Work will start on a new international airport—billed to be Southeast Asia's largest—near Kuala Lumpur.

Capital spending by private industry will slow somewhat in 1993. To improve productivity, companies will step up training and education of personnel.

International trade will maintain healthy levels, with export/import growth estimated at about 12 percent in 1993.

**LANGUAGE**

Bahasa Malaysia is the national language. Because Malaysia is a former British colony, many Malaysians speak and write English. Their English is often spoken with a British accent.

English is widely used in business circles.

**RELIGION**

Islam is the national religion, and Muslims constitute about 53 percent of the population. Other prominent religions are Buddhism (about 17 percent), Taoism and Confucianism (about 12 percent), and Christianity (about 3 percent).

**VITAL ECONOMIC STATISTICS (1991 Estimates)**

| | |
|---|---|
| Population: | 18 million |
| Gross Domestic Product | US$ 47 billion |
| Income Per Capita | US$ 2,600 |
| Annual Growth Rate | 8.3 percent |
| Total Imports | US$ 34.6 billion |
| Total Exports | US$ 34.5 billion |
| U.S. Share of Manufactured Imports | 17 percent |
| U.S. Share of Total Exports | 15.4 percent |

**Top Five Imports From U.S.**

Electronic components and parts
Aircraft
Ferrous waste and scrap
Automatic data processing machines and parts
Oscilloscopes, spectrum analyzers

**Top Five Exports To U.S.**

Electronic components and parts
Telecommunications equipment
Television receivers and combinations
Consumer electronics
Apparel

**Top Three Foreign Investors**

Japan
Taiwan
Singapore

**Top Three Trading Partners**

Japan
Singapore
U.S.

## BEST EXPORT OPPORTUNITIES FOR AMERICAN FIRMS*

**Telecommunications Equipment**  Radar/satellite equipment and services, cellular and stationary telephones, switching and cabling

**Computer Software and Services**  Mini and mainframe software, PC local area network software

**Oil and Gas Equipment**  Exploration equipment, drilling equipment

**Electronic Components**  Semiconductor devices and diodes, electrical integrated circuits and micro assemblies

**Computers and Peripherals**  Mini and micro computers, PCs, mainframes, supercomputers, bar coding equipment

**Industrial Chemicals**  Organo-inorganic and hetesocyclic compounds, nucleic acids and salts, carboxylic acids and derivatives, inorganic chemical elements, oxides and halogen salts

**Defense Equipment**  Arms and ammunition, communications equipment, combat aircraft

**Laboratory Scientific Instruments**  Drawing, marking-out or mathematical calculating instruments, automatic regulating/controlling instruments and apparatus, oscilloscopes, spectrum analyzers and other instruments/apparatus to measure electricity or detect radiation

**Medical Equipment**  Microscopes and parts, surgical appliances, catheters and cabbykae, mechano-therapy equipment, hospital furniture, spectrometers and spectrophotometers

**Iron and Steel**  Ferrous waste and scrap

**Pollution Control Equipment**  For sewerage, industrial effluent, air pollution

**Electronics Industry Production/Test Equipment**  Wafer fabrication equipment, integrated circuit tester

**Aircraft and Parts**  Commercial airplanes

**Industrial Process Controls**  For oil and gas production/processing plants, petrochemical plants, power plants

**Drugs and Pharmaceutical Preparations**  Medicaments containing antibiotics; provitamins and vitamins

---

* U.S. Department of Commerce 1992 Rankings

| | |
|---|---|
| **Pumps, Valves, and Compressors** | Pumps for dispensing fuel or lubricants, centrifugal pumps, compressors in sealed units for refrigerating equipment, pressure-reducing valves |
| **Cosmetics and Toiletries** | Beauty and make-up products, perfume and toilet waters, preparations for oral and dental hygiene |
| **Management Services** | Finance/accounting services, research and development services, feasibility studies, market research, computer consultancy |
| **Food Processing and Packaging Equipment** | For bakery, fat/oil, confectionery products |
| **Electrical Power Systems** | Boilers, turbines, transformers |
| **Plastics Production Machinery** | Injection-molding machines, extrusion machines, blow molding machines, vacuum molding and thermoforming machines |
| **Water Resources Equipment** | Water treatment plants, sewage treatment plants, process control instruments, fluid meters and counting meters, irrigation well drilling equipment, water well drilling equipment, water pipes and fittings ductile |
| **Paper and Paperboard** | Newsprint, uncoated paper and paperboard, coated and impregnated paper and paperboard |
| **Construction Equipment** | Bulldozers, angeldozers, graders and levelers, mechanical shovels, excavators, shovel loaders |
| **Sporting Goods** | Golf equipment, golf balls, gymnasium equipment |
| **Plastics Materials and Resins** | Ethylene polymers, styrene polymers |
| **Non-Ferrous Metals** | Copper, aluminum, zinc |
| **Printing and Graphic Arts Equipment** | Offset printing machinery, machines for printing repetitive designs and wording |
| **Books and Periodicals** | Books, brochures, leaflets, dictionaries, encyclopedias, newspapers, journals, periodicals |
| **Automotive Parts** | Suspension shock-absorbers, clutches, and parts |

## BUSINESS PRACTICES

**Meetings**

Business is conducted in Malaysia with a fair amount of formality. Appointments should be arranged well in advance. It is helpful, but not always necessary, to arrange appointments through personal introductions. Offices of the Malaysian Industrial Development Authority in New York City, Chicago, and Los Angeles can be helpful in setting up appointments in Malaysia for Americans.

Punctuality is important in Malaysia, and it is a good idea to send presentation materials (which can be in English) in advance of a meeting. Do not plan to launch into business discussions immediately, however. Start with social conversation and gradually move to business subjects. Allow plenty of time to conclude your business in Malaysia.

Business discussions are often held over lunch or dinner.

**Business Hours**   Offices normally are open six days a week, Monday through Saturday, with weekday hours from 8 a.m. to 4:30 p.m. and Saturday hours from 8 a.m. to 12:30 p.m. A lunch hour usually is taken around 1 p.m.

**Greetings**   Shaking hands (lightly, not firmly) is now common in business circles in Malaysia for men and women. A Malay person will sometimes extend both hands, grasping both hands of the other person.

**Business Cards**   Always exchange business cards on first meeting. They need not be printed in Bahasa Malaysia on one side. Use cards of good quality. (You will notice that Malaysian business cards are often of exceptionally high quality.)

**Names and Titles**   Malaysian names are a considerable challenge for Americans. Chinese Malaysians normally place the family name first (as in Li Kuo-shu, whose family name is Li), but they sometimes reverse the order if they deal frequently with Westerners. A Malay's principal name (not necessarily a family name) also is normally placed first, followed by an indication of the father's name. For example, Isa bin Jamari is Isa "the son of" Jamari.

As many members of Malaysian royalty and officialdom are active in business, Americans need to be aware of titles that appear as part of a person's name. "Tunku" and "Tengku" are comparable to prince or princess. "Tun," "Tan Sri," and "Dato'" (or "Datuk") are, in descending order, titles of high ranking male officials. "Toh Puan," "Puan Sri," and "Datin" are titles given their wives. "Haji" in a name indicates that the person, a Muslim, has made a pilgrimage to Mecca. The equivalents of "Mr." and "Ms.," respectively, in Bahasa Malaysia are "Encik" and "Cik" (or "Puan" in the case of an older woman).

Americans will find it useful to know these things, but except for addressing royalty and officials it usually is enough simply to use "Mr." or "Ms." in English. If in doubt, ask a Malaysian colleague how to address a certain person, or ask the person directly.

**Clothing**   Visitors to Malaysia should dress for warm weather. Lying just north of the equator, Malaysia is warm and humid. For men, a white shirt and tie are normal, and safari-style suits are popular. A dress or a blouse with skirt is normal for women. Men often wear a jacket to a formal meeting, then take it off during the meeting.

Long sleeved, open neck shirts for men and long sleeved dresses for women are acceptable in the evening. Those made of colorful (but not too bright or loud) batik are popular with Malaysians and can be purchased locally and worn by Americans.

**Gifts and Entertainment**

Business gifts are appreciated but not expected in Malaysia. Gifts from your organization or your part of the United States are the most appropriate. Pens and photo books are always appropriate. Gifts to Muslims should be presented with the right hand, never the left hand. The left hand is the "unclean" hand, used at the toilet.

Business entertaining is common, often in hotels and sometimes in Malaysians' homes. If you are entertained at a Malaysian's home, you should take the hostess a gift, such as candy, cookies, or flowers (but not wine or liquor if the family is Muslim). You should also remove your shoes at the door. If their schedules permit, Americans who are entertained during their visit should reciprocate before returning home.

**Conversation**

Malaysians enjoy talking about family-related subjects, travels, sports, and international affairs. They are warm and interesting people who are good conversationalists. Americans should avoid political and religious topics, although political events in the United States can be freely discussed.

**Hotels**

There are many fine hotels in Kuala Lumpur and elsewhere in Malaysia, but reservations should be made well in advance. Service and dining are especially good.

**Exercise**

Jogging and walking are good exercise activities in Malaysia. Because of the warm weather, such activities should be confined to early morning or evening. Hotels normally have swimming pools and other exercise facilities. Standard athletic wear is acceptable attire for men. Out of respect for conservative Islamic religious beliefs, however, women's attire should not be too brief or revealing.

**Transportation and Communications**

Taxis are the best transportation in Malaysian cities. They normally are plentiful, and fares are reasonable. (If there is no meter, bargain for the fare before the ride begins.) When transportation is needed outside the cities or for several destinations, consider hiring a car and driver for the day. Your hotel can make the arrangements.

Telecommunications are excellent in the better hotels in Kuala Lumpur and in most business offices. Fax machines are in wide use there and international courier services are available. Communications are good to excellent elsewhere in Malaysia.

**Special Considerations**

Malaysian business people are predominantly Chinese Malaysians. However, people of different ethnic backgrounds often work in the same organization. Although women are not normally active in business in Malaysia, there are many women in high positions in government and the professions.

Americans are well advised to be aware that the attitudes of the Malaysian government are conservative. Criticism of the government by the media and others is not tolerated. Materials considered pornographic (even the likes of *Playboy* magazine) are confiscated by customs officials. Convicted drug traffickers are put to death.

The Islamic religion in Malaysia also is conservative. Muslims take their religion very seriously. Muslim women often wear head scarves.

Women of other religions, including visiting American women, are expected to cover their heads and bare arms in mosques.

Malaysians, like Indonesians, are sensitive to gestures and body contact. Americans should generally avoid body contact (especially they should not touch a Malay's head), and they should not touch a person or take food with the left hand (the "unclean" hand).

Yellow is the color of royalty in Malaysia. It normally is inappropriate to use yellow gift wrapping paper or to wear yellow to social events where royalty might be present.

## ENTRY REQUIREMENTS

Americans need a passport, sufficient funds for the stay, and a ticket and documents for onward travel. Visas are required for visits of over 90 days.

## MONEY

The ringgit (dollar) is Malaysia's unit of currency, indicated by a M$ sign. Cash is obtained easily at airport currency exchanges on arrival (during the day) and at banks and hotels. Major credit cards are accepted at hotels and larger establishments but not in most shops. International travelers checks are accepted in hotels but not in shops.

One U.S. dollar is equal to about M$2.50.

## TIPPING

Tipping is not common in Malaysia except for persons who perform small services, such as attendants (50 *sen*, or cents, is the usual tip) and porters (usually M$1 per bag). Taxi drivers normally are not tipped, but they are permitted to keep small change. Restaurants usually will add a ten percent service charge to their bills. Special services, such as those of a driver, can be acknowledged with a small gift such as an American pen or photo book.

## MAJOR HOLIDAYS

| | |
|---|---|
| New Year's Day | January 1 |
| Chinese New Year | January/February* |
| Federal Territory Day | February 1 |
| Hari Raya Puasa | March/April* |
| Labor Day | May 1 |
| Wesak Day | May* |
| King's Birthday | June 6 |
| Hari Raya Raji | July* |
| Awal Muharram | July* |
| National Day | August 31 |
| Birthday of Prophet Muhammed | October* |
| Deepavali | October* |
| Christmas Day | December 25 |

Muslims fast during the lunar month immediately preceding Hari Raya Puasa. They tend not to be available for evening functions during that period, although functions after 8 p.m. often are feasible.

* Date varies

**USEFUL PHRASES**

| English | Bahasa Malaysia | Phonetic Pronunciation |
|---|---|---|
| Welcome | Selamat datan | Slah-maht da-tahng |
| Good morning | Selamat pagi | Slah-maht pah-gee |
| Good evening | Selamat petang | Slah-maht puh-tahng |
| Good night | Selamat malam | Slah-maht mah-lahm |
| Good-bye | Selamat tinggal | Slah-maht ting-gahl |
| Yes | Ya | Yah |
| No | Tidak | Tee-dahk |
| Please | Sila or Tolong | See-lah or Toh-long |
| How much? | Berapa? | Buh-rah-pah |
| Thank you | Terima kasih | Tuh-ree-mah cah-see |
| You're welcome | Sama-sama | Sah-mah sah-mah |
| Cheers | Selamat minum | Slah-maht mee-num |
| I don't understand | Saya tidak faham | Sah-yah tee-dahk fah-hahm |

**USEFUL MALAYSIAN CONTACTS**

Ministry of International Trade and Industry
Block 10, Government Office Complex
Jalan Duta
50622 Kuala Lumpur, Malaysia
TELEPHONE: 60*/3-254-0033
FAX: 60-3-255-0827

Malaysian Industrial Development Authority
Wisma Damansara
Jalan Semantan
50720 Kuala Lumpur, Malaysia
TELEPHONE: 60-3-255-3633
FAX: 60-3-255-7970

Malaysian Industrial Development Authority
875 North Michigan Avenue
Chicago, IL 60611
TELEPHONE: 312/787-4532
FAX: 312/787-4769

Malaysian Consul—Commercial Section
630 Third Avenue
New York, NY 10017
TELEPHONE: 212/687-2491
FAX: 212/490-8450

Malaysian Consulate—Commercial Section
World Trade Center Building
350 South Figueroa Street
Los Angeles, CA 90071
TELEPHONE: 213/617-1000
FAX: 213/485-8617

National Chamber of Commerce and Industry of Malaysia
The Tower, Plaza Pekeliling
Jalan Tun Razak
50400 Kuala Lumpur, Malaysia
TELEPHONE: 60-3-238-0278
FAX: 60-3-232-0473

---

\* Malaysia's country code

Malaysian International Chamber of Commerce and Industry
Wisma Damansara
Jalan Semantan
50490 Kuala Lumpur, Malaysia
TELEPHONE: 60-3-254-2117
FAX: 60-3-255-4946

U. S. Embassy
Commercial Section
376 Jalan Tun Razak
50400 Kuala Lumpur, Malaysia
TELEPHONE: 60-3-248-9011
FAX: 60-3-242-1866

American Business Council of Malaysia
Amoda Building
Jalan Imbi
55100 Kuala Lumpur, Malaysia
TELEPHONE: 60-3-242-8540
FAX: 60-3-243-7234

# COUNTRY PROFILE: THE PHILIPPINES

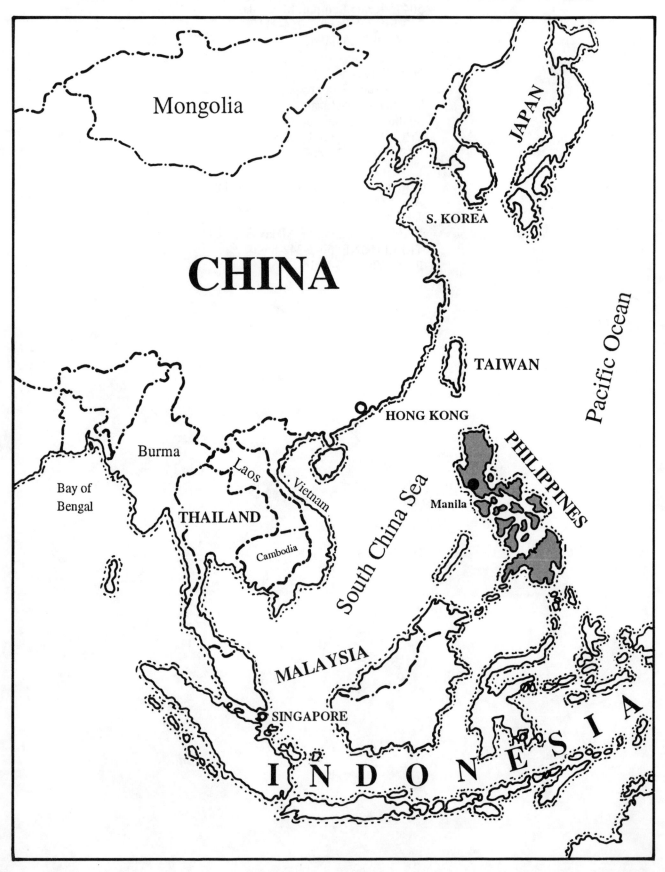

## PIONEERING IN THE PHILIPPINES

Vince Espino and Leon Guinto are naturalized American citizens who came to the United States from the Philippines more than twenty-five years ago and became successful businessmen in New York City. Espino manages a freight forwarding company with an Asia-wide network of offices. Guinto packages computer software systems for client companies. In 1991, armed with an exclusive distributorship agreement for Club Car motorized golf cars, they embarked on an effort to export the cars and various golf accessories to the Philippines. Within a short time, they expanded their plans and by 1994 will be manufacturing golf cars in the Philippines for both domestic and export sales.

"When we first went to the Philippine government for a license to import the golf cars, we found that they were completely banned," says Espino. "The government is trying to build up domestic industry and discourage imports, especially imports of luxury and big ticket items."

"We were dealing with the government's One-Stop Action Center, and they were very helpful," adds Espino. "They told us about the Philippines' new Pioneer Enterprise program. As a result, we've expanded our plans tremendously, and we're very excited about our prospects."

The Pioneer Enterprise program was set up under the Philippines' 1991 Foreign Investments Act. The program awards substantial tax incentives and import duty exemptions to various enterprises that establish manufacturing operations in the Philippines or that are engaged in certain activities deemed vitally important to the country's economic development.

"We registered our company, Club Car Philippines, with the Board of Investments in early 1992," says Espino, president of the new company. "We'll put up our manufacturing facility in 1993 on an industrial estate in Cabuyao in the Province of Laguna. Our plans call for it to have about 10,000 square feet of space and initially about 25 employees. Our deal with the government is that we'll have export sales by June 1993 and in due course export at least 50 percent of our production."

"This venture is no shot in the dark," claims Espino. "Even before we decided to go the manufacturing route, we had a consulting firm do a marketing study on the prospects for sales of golf cars and accessories in the Philippines and several Southeast Asian countries. We also got a lot of helpful information from Aida Miranda at the Commercial Section of the U.S. Embassy in Manila. We're convinced that the demand for golf cars and equipment is really going to take off in the Philippines and Southeast Asia during the 1990s."

"In addition, the Philippine government is letting us get the head start we need," says Espino. "They authorized us to bring in our golf cars knocked down. We assemble them in Manila, display them in our showroom, and then sell them to individuals and country clubs. We also rent golf cars."

Club Car Philippines will always have close ties with the United States, according to Espino. "When we start manufacturing, we will need to import parts and components from the U.S., and we will develop a line of American golf products."

"This project couldn't be better for Leon Guinto and me," adds Espino. "It gives us a chance to give something back to our homeland by generating employment for Filipinos. It also gives us an excuse to play golf more often."

## THE PHILIPPINES: ECONOMIC BACKGROUND

The Philippines and the United States go back a long way together. Technically, all the way back to 1898 when the Spanish ceded the Philippines to the United States following the Spanish-American war. Although the Philippines became independent from the United States in 1946, the two countries maintain close ties. Notwithstanding occasional disagreements, a strong bond exists between them.

For Americans, the Philippines evokes vibrant images: from General Douglas MacArthur's "I shall return!" promise as he and his forces withdrew from Bataan and Corregidor at the beginning of World War II, to the withdrawal of U.S. military forces from Subic Bay and Clark Air Base, to compassion for the damage caused in the Philippines in recent years by earthquakes, typhoons, and volcanic eruptions.

For Filipinos, the United States evokes the feelings that one normally has toward a parent or sibling; often warm, sometimes resentful, always intense.

In many ways, the differences between the Philippines and the United States are striking. The Philippines is a large island nation well on the other side of the world, lying just north of the equator between the South China Sea and the Pacific Ocean. It has over 7,000 islands, with the eleven largest having 94 percent of the country's land area. Luzon, to the north, where Manila is located, is the largest island; Mindanao, to the south, is the next largest. The country's 62 million people are mostly of Malay stock, but there are many ethnic and cultural sub-groups. Seventy percent of the population live in rural areas.

The Philippines' first contact with the Western world came in 1521 with the arrival of Ferdinand Magellan, the Portuguese navigator. (Magellan was killed there by the warrior king Lapu-Lapu.) The Spanish later colonized the Philippines, exerting largely political and religious influences. Philippine trade developed primarily with China and Mexico, with trade ultimately dominated in the nineteenth century by Chinese merchants.

In many ways, the Philippines is the most Western of Asian countries. Christianity, mostly Roman Catholicism, is its principal religion. English is the principal language in business, government, schools, and most communications. (In terms of population, the Philippines is the third largest English-speaking nation in the world, after the United States and England.) As part of the country's "inheritance" from its years as a U.S. possession, many of the laws and governmental systems of the Philippines are similar to those of the United States. There also is an extensive educational system modeled on Western concepts, with over 40 universities and 375 private colleges.

Economically, the Philippines is a country of great potential and a source of substantial opportunity for American exporters and investors. There are abundant natural resources and a large, English-literate work force. While 1991 income per capita was only about US$740, the size of the Philippine population indicates a broad potential for consumer products and services.

On the debit side, political unrest, official corruption, and the vested interests of powerful landed gentries dampen economic reforms in the Philippines, impede trade liberalization, and discourage foreign investment. The Philippines also is energy-dependent, with only about 40 percent of its recent energy requirements being domestically produced. (Huge sums were expended in the mid-1970s to build a 600MW nuclear power plant, but the project never was completed). In addition, its infrastructure—the country's system of roads, for example—is either badly in need of repair or inadequate to meet a rapid expansion of the economy.

Together with Singapore, Indonesia, Malaysia, Thailand, and Brunei, the Philippines is a member of the Association of Southeast Asian Nations (ASEAN). The ASEAN nations collaborate in various ways to promote trade and investment in their region.

For American exporters, the Philippines is potentially a bright star. Filipinos and Americans share a cultural affinity and many commonly held beliefs. The country itself has virtually all of the human and natural resources needed to become a leader in economic development. The United States, Japan, and other industrial nations, with loans and direct foreign investment, are banking heavily on the future of the Philippines. There is strong evidence that Americans who invest their time, money, and effort in the Philippines are not likely to be disappointed.

## NEAR-TERM OUTLOOK

President Fidel Ramos, elected to office in 1992, will consolidate his political base during 1993 and will turn his attention to the country's stagnating economy. Growth will continue to lag behind that of other Southeast Asian nations, but the gross national product will improve nevertheless in 1993, rising about 4 percent. Inflation will abate significantly, from a high of 19 percent in 1991 to around eight percent in 1993.

Trade will improve in 1993, with imports rising 18 percent and exports 15 percent. Further steps will be taken to reduce tariffs and other trade barriers. Foreign investment should increase, attracted by ample low cost labor and a liberalized regulatory framework under the new Foreign Investments Act.

Despite budget deficits, the government will continue work on several high-visibility infrastructure projects, including much-needed highway extensions and interchanges in Metro Manila and additions to the country's power generating capacity.

## LANGUAGE

The official language of the Philippines is Pilipino (a form of the Tagalog dialect), which is used mainly in Metro Manila and by the mass media. English is widely spoken as a first or second language and is the basic language in business, government, and schools. Altogether, there are some 86 spoken languages, the principal ones being Tagalog, Ilocano, and Cebuano.

## RELIGION

The Philippines is about 93 percent Christian, predominantly Roman Catholic. Islam is the principal religion in the southern regions (on Mindanao and in the Sulu archipelago).

## VITAL ECONOMIC STATISTICS (1991 Estimates)

| | |
|---|---|
| Population: | 62.1 million |
| Gross Domestic Product | US$ 45.9 billion |
| Income Per Capita | US$ 739 |
| Annual Growth Rate | 1.7 percent |
| Total Imports | US$ 13 billion |
| Total Exports | US$ 8.7 billion |
| U.S. Share of Manufactured Imports | 7 percent |
| U.S. Share of Total Exports | 29.9 percent |

**Top Five Imports From U.S.**    Materials for garments and semi-conductor manufacture
Non-electric machinery
Transport equipment
Electrical machinery, apparatus, and supplies
Cereal and cereal preparations

**Top Five Exports To U.S.**    Consigned garments and semiconductor devices
Clothing and accessories
Electrical equipment
Fruits and vegetables
Sugar

**Top Three Foreign Investors**    U.S.
Japan
Hong Kong

**Top Three Trading Partners**    U.S.
Japan
Germany

## BEST EXPORT OPPORTUNITIES FOR AMERICAN FIRMS*

**Industrial Chemicals**    Nucleic acids and heterocyclic compounds, styrene, organo-sulfur, lactams, ethers and derivatives, methacrylic acid, its salts and esters, toluene, methyl alcohol, chloroethylene, esters and acetic acid

**Telecommunications Equipment**    Telephone and telex equipment, mobile telecommunications equipment, cellular telecommunications systems, telecommunications accessories

**Building Products**    Portland cement and cement clinker, reinforcing steel, concrete fabricated materials, prefab steel for industrial and commercial buildings, fabricated structural materials

**Plastic Materials and Resins**    Polyethylene, polypropylene, polyvinyl chloride

**Computers and Peripherals**    Peripherals, compatibles and mini-micro computers, business and desk top micros, home/hobby microcomputers

**Mining Industry**    Underground equipment, mineral beneficiation equipment, crushing, pulverizing and screening equipment, mining accessories, mining safety equipment and supplies

**Hotel and Restaurant Equipment**    Cold storage equipment, specialized equipment, bakery equipment, food service equipment

**Security and Safety Equipment**    Safety, rescue, communications, and surveillance equipment, military equipment, alarms and signals, electronic detection equipment, fire protection equipment, specialized safety and security equipment

---

* U.S. Chamber of Commerce 1992 Rankings

| | |
|---|---|
| **Medical Equipment** | X-ray machines, computerized medical equipment, ultrasound and scanners, surgical equipment, medical supplies, therapeutic equipment, monitoring equipment |
| **Food Processing and Packaging Equipment** | Bakery equipment, meat processing equipment, juice processing equipment, wrapping and packaging equipment, bottling machinery |
| **Architectural, Construction, and Engineering Services** | Engineering design, petrochemical engineering design, construction and mining engineering design, architectural design and management |
| **Pollution Control Systems** | Water and wastewater pollution control systems, surface aerators, paddle wheel aerators, differential flow systems, rotary biological contactors and pumps, solid waste management systems, compacting and transfer equipment, arm container rollers, compactor and dump trucks, spare parts and technical services |
| **Electrical Power Systems** | Transmission and distribution equipment, generation equipment |
| **Electronic Components** | Semiconductor devices, including integrated circuits, printed circuits, piezoelectric crystals |
| **Printing and Graphic Arts Equipment** | Folding machines, paper cutters, sheet fed/web offset, multicolored computerized systems, printers, reproduction cameras and scanners, printing accessories |
| **Household Consumer Goods** | House wares and household appliances, hand and power tools |
| **Laboratory Instruments** | Chemical and physical analysis instruments, replacement parts |
| **Renewable Energy Resources** | Biomass energy systems from ricehull, coconut shell, bagasse and agri-waste, biogas systems from manure, solar energy systems for households and commercial buildings, photo voltaic systems for rural electrification and telecommunications |
| **Avionics and Ground Support Equipment** | Airborne avionics equipment, ground-based avionics equipment |
| **Automotive Parts and Components** | Knocked-down chassis and frames for trucks, buses, and cars, motor vehicle instruments, vehicle bodies, diesel and semi-diesel engines and parts, transmissions |
| **Computer Software** | Database management systems, local area networks, custom package software development, application programs for local and foreign firms |

## BUSINESS PRACTICES

### Meetings

Business appointments in the Philippines should be arranged long in advance (if possible, one month ahead if you are traveling from overseas), preferably through someone who knows both you and the party with whom you will meet. A Philippine government office or a consultant can assist in making appointments, but a business colleague is best.

Business is conducted with reasonable formality, but it is essential to begin with social conversation before proceeding to business topics.

Despite a relaxed approach to social engagements in the Philippines, punctuality is important when it comes to business. Allow plenty of time to conclude your business. Once a meeting begins, it should not be rushed.

**Business Hours**

Offices are normally open five days a week, Monday through Friday, from 8 a.m. to 5 p.m., with a lunch hour from noon to 1 p.m. Some offices are open on Saturday morning from 8 a.m. to noon.

**Greetings**

Filipino business people — men and women — greet each other by shaking hands (lightly, not firmly). Americans should do the same, but should give women the option of extending the hand first.

**Business Cards**

Business cards should be exchanged on first meeting. Your regular cards will do since cards in the Philippines are normally printed in English.

**Names and Titles**

In formal settings and meetings, professionals and senior Philippine officials in government and business should be addressed with their titles, as in "Chairman Monsod," "Ambassador Mutuc," "Engineer Ramos," and "Professor Montes." They also may be addressed as "Sir" or "Ma'am." With peers and in informal settings, it is usually enough simply to use "Mr.," "Ms.," or "Dr.," as appropriate. After a close association develops, it is permissible to use first names.

**Clothing**

Business people in the Philippines dress well. Despite the warm weather, men should wear a jacket and tie to business meetings, and women should wear a dress or blouse with skirt or pants. Jackets are often doffed during meetings if temperatures are warm. In informal meetings, Filipino men often wear short sleeved barongs, Philippine shirts of cotton and polyester with some embroidery, not tucked in at the waist.

In the evenings, at restaurants and other public places, a jacket and tie for a man and a dress for a woman are the most appropriate. In lieu of a jacket, Filipino men often wear a long sleeved barong, normally one made of pineapple fiber and with considerable embroidery.

American men who anticipate lengthy or repeated visits to the Philippines should consider purchasing one or more barongs. They are very comfortable, and they will indicate to Filipinos your interest in their country.

**Gifts and Entertainment**

Business gifts are appropriate in the Philippines when important relationships are involved. Otherwise they are not necessary or expected. As in other countries, the best gifts are those associated with your organization or your part of the United States, such as a pen with your company's logo or a book of photographs about your city. Other good gifts are liquor (unless the person is Muslim) or a subscription to an American business magazine.

Filipino business people often entertain visiting Americans at restaurants and in their homes. If you are entertained at home, you should take the hostess a gift, such as cakes or fruits (but not wine or liquor if the family is Muslim). Americans who are entertained during their visit should reciprocate before returning home, especially if business dealings have been successful. American business women, however, are not expected to entertain Filipino businessmen.

**Conversation**    Filipinos are very family-oriented. They enjoy talking about family-related subjects, and they will ask many questions about an American's family and personal life. Food, clothing, and other lifestyle topics are also of interest, but Americans should avoid raising political or religious issues. Since some Filipinos are resentful of United States policies, issues such as foreign aid and the U.S. military presence in Asia should be avoided. Criticism and complaints on any subject also should be avoided.

**Hotels**    Manila has many fine hotels, and there are good hotels elsewhere in the Philippines. Reservations should be made well in advance. Hotel service and dining generally are excellent. Hotels normally are the best places for Americans to do business entertaining in the Philippines.

**Exercise**    Except during business hours in business districts, the streets of Manila can be unsafe for American visitors. Therefore, jogging and walking should be confined to your hotel grounds or, in the company of others, to areas or parks adjacent to your hotel. Warm weather makes early morning or evening the best time for exercise. Hotels also normally have swimming pools and other exercise facilities. Standard athletic wear, including shorts, is acceptable attire for men and women.

**Transportation and Communications**    Traffic is congested in Philippine cities, especially in Manila. Allow plenty of time to get where you are going.

Taxis are the best form of transportation in the cities. Select taxis with meters, if possible. If a taxi has no meter, bargain for the fare before the ride begins. It is also a good idea to ask a hotel doorman, or office building doorman, to give directions to the driver and, if there is no meter, to arrange the fare.

When transportation is needed outside the cities or for several destinations, consider hiring a car and driver for the day. Your hotel can make the arrangements.

Telecommunications are good in the better hotels in Manila and in most business offices. Fax machines are in wide use there and international courier services are available. Communications are only fair elsewhere in the Philippines. To avoid delays and hotel surcharges, it is a good idea to arrange for your office or home to place calls to you at appointed times.

**Special Considerations**

Although Filipinos are Westernized in many ways, their cultural traditions are collectivist rather than individualist. Americans should anticipate that their Filipino business associates will value group goals and long-term relationships more highly than personal goals and short-term results. They also will emphasize harmony, politeness, and modesty more highly than their American counterparts. Hierarchical positions are closely observed, and older people are accorded special deference.

Americans who visit the Philippines will enjoy the country's arts and cultural activities. Theaters and museums abound, and Manila's night life is famous for its music and entertainment.

As mentioned above, city streets are not always safe for visiting Americans. Theft, pick pocketing, and burglary are prevalent in some parts of Philippine cities and on public conveyances. Therefore, you should avoid side streets and remote areas and take more than the usual precautions to guard your personal belongings: lock the windows of your room when going out, place special valuables in a hotel safe (and get an itemized receipt), and wear a money belt if walking in crowded areas.

## ENTRY REQUIREMENTS

Americans on business need a passport, a letter of guarantee from their company, a visa, sufficient funds for the stay, and a ticket and documents for onward travel.

## MONEY

The Philippines' unit of currency is the peso, indicated by a P sign. Cash is easily obtained at airport currency exchanges on arrival (during the day) and at banks and hotels. Major credit cards are accepted at hotels and larger establishments but not in most shops. International travelers checks are accepted at hotels and banks but rarely elsewhere.

One U.S. dollar is equal to about P25.

## TIPPING

Tipping is normally appropriate in the Philippines only for persons who perform small services, such as washroom attendants (5 pesos) and doormen and porters (10 to 20 pesos). Taxi drivers usually are not tipped unless the trip is for an hour or more, when they are tipped ten percent of the fare. Hotels and restaurants will usually add a ten percent service charge to their bills. (If a restaurant does not add the service charge, you should leave a ten percent tip.) Special services, such as those of a driver, can be acknowledged with a small gift such as a cassette tape of an American entertainer.

## MAJOR HOLIDAYS

| | |
|---|---|
| New Year's Day | January 1 |
| Maundy Thursday | Thursday before Easter |
| Good Friday | Friday before Easter |
| Easter | March/April* |
| Bataan and Corregidor Day | April 9 |
| Labor Day | May 1 |
| Independence Day | June 12 |
| National Heroes Day | Last Sunday of August |
| All Saints' Day | November 1 |
| Bonifacio Day | November 30 |
| Christmas Day | December 25 |
| Rizal Day | December 30 |
| Last day of the year | December 31 |

## USEFUL PHRASES

| English | Tagalog | Phonetic Pronunciation |
|---|---|---|
| Hello | Kumasta | Koom-ah-stah |
| Good morning | Magandang umaga po | Ma-gahn-dahng oo-mah-gah po |
| Good afternoon | Magandang hapon po | Ma-gahn-dahng ha-poan po |

* Date varies

| English | Tagalog | Phonetic Pronunciation |
|---|---|---|
| Good evening | Magandang gabi po | Ma-gahn-dahng ga-bee po |
| Good-bye | Paalam | Pa-ah-lahm |
| Yes | Opo | O-po |
| No | Hindi po | Heen-dee po |
| Please | Paki | Pah-key |
| How much? | Maghano ba ito? | Mahg-hah-no bah eetoh |
| Thank you | Salamat po | Sah-lah-maht po |
| You're welcome | Walang anu man | Wah-lahng ah-noo mahn |
| Cheers | Mabuhay | Mah-boo-hay |
| I don't understand (Please repeat) | Paki ulit po | Pah-key oo-lit po |

**USEFUL PHILIPPINE CONTACTS**

Department of Trade and Industry
Board of Investments Building
385 Senator Gil J. Puyat Avenue
Makati, Metro Manila, The Philippines
TELEPHONE: 63*/2-816-0121
FAX: 63-2-816-0552

One-Stop Action Center
Board of Investments Building
385 Gil J. Puyat Avenue
Makati, Metro Manila, The Philippines
TELEPHONE: 63-2-818-1831
FAX: 63-2-819-1887

Philippine Chamber of Commerce and Industries
ODC International Plaza Building
219 Salcedo Street, Legaspi Village
Makati, Metro Manila, The Philippines
TELEPHONE: 63-2-817-6981
FAX: 63-3-816-1946

U. S. Embassy
Commercial Section
395 Senator Gil J. Puyat Avenue
Makati, Metro Manila, The Philippines
TELEPHONE: 63-2-818-6674
FAX: 63-2-818-2684

American Chamber of Commerce
Corinthian Plaza, Paseo de Roxas, Legaspi Village
Makati, Metro Manila, The Philippines
TELEPHONE: 63-2-818-7911
FAX: 63-2-816-6359

---

* Philipines' country code

# COUNTRY PROFILE: SINGAPORE

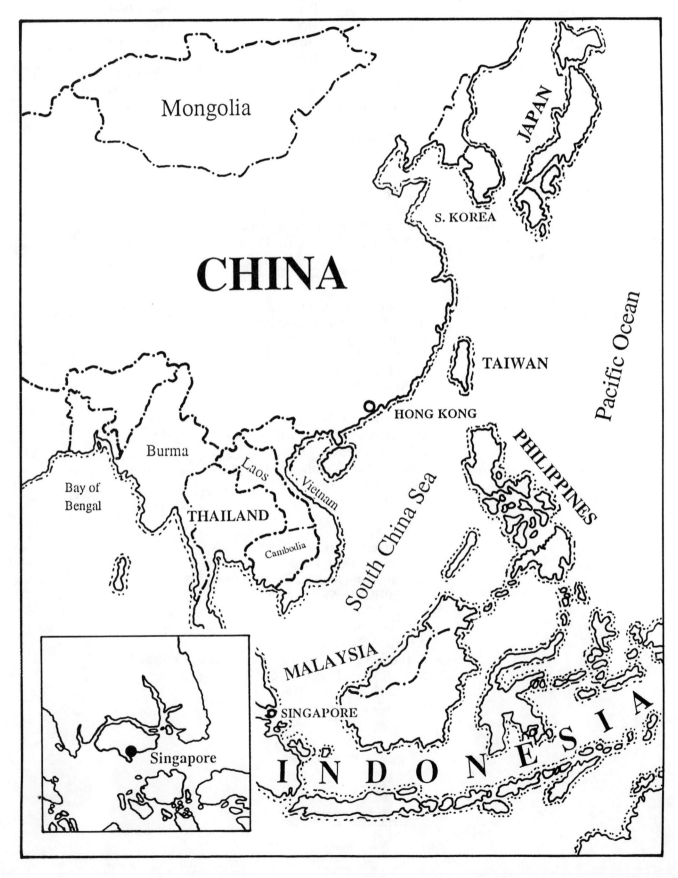

## SINGAPORE SYNERGY

"American companies that want to participate in Asian markets had better get involved now, because by the year 2000 they won't be needed," according to Treva Dvorak, Marketing Manager of Laboratory Tops, Inc., of Taylor, Texas. "Right now, American technology and know-how produce plenty of market opportunities for U.S. firms," she claims, "but Asia is developing so rapidly that these advantages will disappear by the end of the 1990s."

Laboratory Tops jumped into Asia for the first time in 1989 and is now selling its products in Singapore, Malaysia, South Korea, Taiwan, and Japan. The company manufactures and fabricates chemical resistant epoxy resin counter tops, sinks, and accessories for use in laboratory environments where harsh chemicals are present. Formed in 1970, Laboratory Tops has 167 employees and annual sales in excess of $12 million.

"Singapore is an important market for us because so much is being spent there on research and medical facilities," says Dvorak. "Also, most products enter Singapore duty free, which means that Singapore is a gateway to other Asian markets as well."

"American products have a good reputation there, which is a tremendous advantage," adds Dvorak.

Dvorak credits the U.S. Department of Commerce and the Texas Department of Commerce for helping Laboratory Tops to get started in Asia. These agencies provided contacts and information for the company's initial market entries.

"Trade shows have proven to be the best way for us to introduce our products in Asia." says Dvorak. "In Singapore, we participated in the 1991 Chemical Instrument Analab Trade Show. This is a large regional show that draws key players from all over Asia."

A trade show is the first step in selecting a distributor or representative, according to Dvorak. "After an initial contact at our trade show booth, we visit a prospective distributor at its office. This gives us a chance to size up its operations. If we're impressed, we ask to accompany the distributor on one or more sales calls in order to get a feel for the extent and quality of its client base. Then we're ready to make a decision."

"Distributors always want an exclusive," says Dvorak. "We resist this, but it's sometimes hard to avoid, especially in South Korea and Taiwan. Our opening position is, 'We'll consider an exclusive after we've seen what you can do.'"

Dvorak has not found language to be a barrier. English is spoken by business people wherever she goes in Asia. "We normally staff our trade show booth with an interpreter," says Dvorak, "but this is more of a cultural courtesy than a necessity."

The fact that Dvorak is a woman executive dealing mostly with Asian men is also not a problem. "I don't hide my femininity. For me, it's not an issue," says Dvorak.

Once distributors are selected, the key to Laboratory Tops success in Asia has been in demonstrating sincere interest, commitment, and prompt service response. "We provide installation and maintenance videos and manuals, including some translated literature. We try to solve our customers' problems, whatever they are. And it's our policy that every inquiry gets a response within 24 hours," says Dvorak.

Dvorak's advice to American firms: "Come on in, the water's fine. Just plan to work hard and be patient. Things take time in Asia."

## SINGAPORE: ECONOMIC BACKGROUND

Singapore lays just claim to being the "Economic Miracle" of Southeast Asia. In less than thirty years, since leaving the Malaysian federation in 1965 to become an independent republic, Singapore has forged one of the strongest economies in Asia, one boasting the highest per capita income—after Japan—in Asia.

A visitor to Singapore is immediately impressed with its brisk efficiency. Its airport is one of the best in the world, with travelers in and out of it so fast they barely notice. Visitors are whisked into the city by taxis along attractive, tree-lined highways, arriving at one of many modern hotels within a half hour. During their stay, they will be impressed with Singapore's modern office buildings, new subway system, cleanliness, and fine dining.

A visitor also will soon discern the key to Singapore's economic success: a visionary, hands-on government that leaves nothing to chance and involves itself deeply in the affairs and welfare of its people. This is no helter-skelter growth economy. Citizens are told what to do and when and where to do it. For example, voting is compulsory, saving a part of one's salary is mandatory, and long hair on men is officially discouraged. While visiting business people are guests and are treated like valued customers, they too need to follow certain rules and regulations.

In sharp contrast to its economic weight, the Republic of Singapore is a small nation, consisting of the island of Singapore and some 57 smaller islands at the southern tip of Peninsular Malaysia. Its population is just over three million and its aggregate land area is less than one-fifth the size of Rhode Island, the United States' smallest state.

In many ways, Singapore is similar to Hong Kong. It too is an island city state founded on a trading economy. Although its population is ethnically mixed, it too is largely Chinese. 78 percent of its people are ethnic Chinese. The remaining ethnic groups are Malay (14 percent), Indian (seven percent), and "other" (one percent).

Founded in 1819 as a trading post for the British East India Company by Sir Stamford Raffles, Singapore is now the modern essence of its origin: a technology-oriented manufacturing, financial, and services center that is the trading hub of Southeast Asia. It is strategically located at the geographical heart of the region, adjacent to the Straits of Malacca, and has a large deep-water harbor. There are virtually no trade barriers. More than 3,000 American, Japanese, and European multinational organizations—including Exxon, General Motors, Glaxo, and Hewlett-Packard—maintain regional offices and operations there. One-third of U.S. multinational investment in Singapore is in electronics manufacturing and assembly.

Except for three years of Japanese occupation during World War II, British control continued until Singapore first became self-governing in 1959. The British influence is still felt. English, spoken with a British accent, is the principal language of business, government, and education. The legal and governmental systems are based on those of the British.

During the 1970s and 1980s, Singapore's economic growth was export-driven. A large manufacturing sector was established on the basis of an ample, educated work force and liberal foreign investment policies. In recent years, Singapore's economic success produced a tight labor supply and higher wages. As a result, the government has shifted its economic policies to discourage investment in labor-intensive activities and promote technology-based value-added manufacturing.

Singapore also established, with Indonesia and the Malaysian state of Johor, an offshore "Growth Triangle" to attract foreign investment to its immediate neighbors, thereby enhancing its own position as a trading and financial center. The "Growth Triangle" was established in Indonesia's Riau Island group (primarily on Batam Island), just south of Singapore. It aims to take advantage of low cost labor and land in the Riau island group, low cost but skilled labor in Johor, and the financial and technological resources of Singapore. The governments involved collaborated smoothly to promote the concept and to install infrastructure and industrial parks on Batam Island. A number of manufacturing facilities for electronics, garments, plastics, and other products are already in operation there.

Singapore's economic policies now focus on strengthening its role as Southeast Asia's primary commercial and financial center in an "Age of Information and Technology." Fittingly, its financial services sector has been its growth leader in recent years, and high-tech manufacturing continues to advance. In addition, Singapore's growing wealth has enabled it to expand its economic base with direct foreign investment elsewhere, in its "Growth Triangle" and in other countries.

Americans should consider Singapore not only an important market but also a good place from which to establish business connections in Asia, especially Southeast Asia. Although Singapore's population base is small, Singaporeans have a high standard of living (1991 per capita income is over $13,000) and a strong appetite for American products and services. There is a high literacy rate. As a trading center with modern infrastructure and communication systems, Singapore provides many opportunities for Americans to connect with expanding markets throughout Asia.

**Near-Term Outlook** Singapore's economy, highly dependent on international trade, took something of a beating during the world economic slowdown of 1990-1992, falling from double digit growth in the late 1980s to six percent in 1992. Growth will improve to seven percent or better in 1993, with inflation holding at around three percent.

Labor shortages will remain a nagging problem, putting upward pressure on wage rates. Despite higher per capita income, however, consumer spending will increase only a moderate five percent.

Private industry, prodded by government policy, will spend heavily on development of technology-based value-added manufacturing. The government will continue to spend heavily on infrastructure, notably telecommunications and renovation of Singapore's extensive public housing facilities.

Exports and imports are projected to grow by 12 percent in 1993.

**LANGUAGE**

Singapore's official languages are English, Chinese (Mandarin), Malay, and Tamil. However, English is the principal language of business and government and is widely used throughout Singapore. Several Chinese dialects are spoken (Hokkien, Teochew, Cantonese, Hainanese, Hakka and Foochow), but the government encourages the use of Mandarin in place of these dialects.

**RELIGION**

There is tolerance toward all religions in Singapore and many are practiced. The majority of the population is Buddhist, Confucian, and Taoist. There also are many Muslims, Hindus, and Christians.

**VITAL ECONOMIC STATISTICS (1991 Estimates)**

| | |
|---|---|
| Population: | 3.1 million |
| Gross Domestic Product | US$ 40.2 billion |
| Income Per Capita | US$ 13,135 |
| Annual Growth Rate | 7.5 percent |
| Total Imports | US$ 69.1 billion |
| Total Exports | US$ 61.5 billion |
| U.S. Share of Manufactured Imports | 18 percent |
| U.S. Share of Total Exports | 19 percent |

**Top Five Imports From U.S.**

Microcircuits
Chemicals
Data processing machines
Aircraft
Computers

**Top Five Exports To U.S.**

Data processing machines
Integrated circuits
Apparel
Parts for office machines and data processing machines
Telecommunications equipment

**Top Three Foreign Investors**

U.S.
Japan
Europe

**Top Three Trading Partners**

U.S.
Japan
Malaysia

**BEST EXPORT OPPORTUNITIES FOR AMERICAN FIRMS***

**Electronic Components**

**Computer Software and Services**   Application software, business and financial software

**Computers and Peripherals**   Minicomputers, workstations, microcomputers, tapes, disks for computers

---

* U.S Chamber of Commerce 1992 Rankings

| | |
|---|---|
| **Pollution Control Equipment** | Filtering and purifying machinery, laboratory equipment, incinerators |
| **Avionics and Ground Support Equipment** | Aircraft ground support and aircraft system repairing equipment |
| **Laboratory and Scientific Instruments** | Analytical and scientific instruments |
| **Telecommunications Equipment** | Transmission equipment and products, cellular mobile radio and paging systems, data communication equipment |
| **Oil and Gas Field Machinery and Services** | Valves, spare parts |
| **Electronics Industry Production and Test Equipment** | Fabrication equipment, test equipment, circuit packaging equipment |
| **Building Products** | Human environment controlling sensors |
| **Pumps, Valves, and Compressors** | Heat exchangers and pumps |
| **Audio/Visual Equipment** | Audio/visual equipment, tapes |
| **Medical Equipment and Products** | Operating room equipment, general hospital equipment, medical disposable products |
| **Air-Conditioning and Refrigeration Equipment** | Air conditioners, refrigerators, and freezers |
| **Materials Handling Machinery** | Lifting and handling equipment, jacks and hoists, lifts and skip hoists |
| **Robotics and Industrial Automation Equipment** | Programmable controllers, manipulating machinery and equipment |
| **Aviation/Helicopter Services** | Facilities management, air traffic control, pilot training |
| **Machine Tools and Metalworking Equipment** | Metal cutting and metal forming machine tools |
| **Printing and Graphic Arts Equipment** | Typemaking and typesetting machines, photographic equipment for graphics, binding and cutting machines |
| **Hotel and Restaurant Equipment** | Tableware and kitchenware, food preparation equipment |
| **Household Consumer Goods** | Tableware and kitchenware, cooking apparatus and domestic food preparation equipment, sanitary ware, tap fittings and bathroom accessories, textile furnishings and carpets, household kitchen appliances |
| **Processed Foods** | Ready-to-eat and prepared ingredients |

| | |
|---|---|
| **Biotechnology** | Test equipment, chemicals |
| **Process Controls, Industrial** | Sensing and measuring instruments, electronic data processing equipment |
| **Sporting Goods** | Golf equipment |
| **Health Care Services** | Hospital management services |
| **Food Processing and Packaging Equipment** | Filling and packaging equipment, automated food processing equipment |
| **Aircraft and Parts** | |
| **Cosmetics and Toiletries** | Skin care, perfumes |
| **Dental Equipment** | Instruments and apparatus for dental use |

## BUSINESS PRACTICES

**Meetings**

Business meetings in Singapore are straightforward and no-nonsense events. Nonetheless, meetings should start with social conversation. Formalities and relationships are important in business, so it is advisable for Americans to arrange their appointments well in advance through an intermediary who knows both parties. A consultant, bank, colleague, or government office can make these arrangements.

Be punctual and well prepared for any meeting. Singaporeans have a reputation for being sharp business people. Plan on discussing business points in great detail. Allow plenty of time to complete a business transaction.

Business discussions are frequently held over lunch but not normally over breakfast or dinner.

**Business Hours**

Offices are normally open six days a week, Monday through Friday from 9 a.m. to 5 p.m., and on Saturday from 9 a.m. to 1 p.m. A lunch hour is taken on weekdays from 1 p.m. to 2 p.m.

**Greetings**

Shaking hands is the usual greeting for men and women in business settings in Singapore. This often is combined with a slight bow when greeting ethnic Chinese people.

**Business Cards**

Americans should present their business cards on first meeting. Cards need not be printed in Chinese on one side since English is one of Singapore's official languages and is normally used in business.

**Names and Titles**

The ethnic Chinese, who constitute the bulk of the business community in Singapore, normally place their family name first. Thus, the surname of a man named Lim Lee Chen would be Lim. However, contrary to Chinese tradition, those who are in frequent contact with the international business community sometimes place their surnames last, Western style.

Titles are not normally important in Singapore. People usually are addressed as "Mr.," "Dr.," or "Ms." as appropriate. First names, however, are not appropriate unless a close association has developed.

**Clothing**

As Singapore is warm and humid, the usual business attire is shirts and ties for men and blouses with skirts or pants for women. Safari-style suits are also popular with Singaporean men, and American men who are frequent visitors to Singapore often wear them as well. In the evening, men may need a jacket for some restaurants. Women often wear dresses in the evening.

**Gifts and Entertainment**

Gift-giving is not common in Singapore unless a close association has been developed. Gifts on first meetings tend to be considered bribes to establish a relationship.

After a close business relationship develops, gift-giving is appropriate on suitable occasions, such as the signing of a contract or the anniversary of a partnership. Good gifts are those associated with your organization or your part of the United States.

Business entertaining is also not appropriate at first. Americans should let their Singaporean colleagues be the first to extend a dinner invitation. They should then reciprocate before returning to the United States, if possible.

Government officials are not permitted to accept gifts or business entertainment. It is sometimes possible, however, to meet socially with officials over "Dutch-treat" business luncheons and other occasions when the expense is shared.

**Conversation**

Singaporeans, like other Asians from collectivist cultures, are always interested in matters involving their families and organizations and those of others. They will want to know all about you and your family and organization, and they will enjoy talking about their own. They also are patriotic people and they enjoy discussing Singapore's achievements. However, political topics are especially sensitive and should not be raised by visitors. Other good topics of conversation are international business (since Singapore is now heavily involved in global economic affairs) and the perennials—food, prices, and shopping.

**Hotels**

Singapore has many fine hotels with excellent service, facilities, and dining. Reserve in advance as you would do normally.

**Exercise**

There are a number of good opportunities for exercise in Singapore. There are roads and parks that are excellent (and safe) for jogging and walking, although warm and humid weather confines these activities to the early morning and evening. Many hotels have swimming pools and other exercise facilities. There also are health centers and private clubs with exercise facilities to which visitors might gain access through their Singaporean friends.

Standard athletic wear, including shorts, is acceptable attire for men and women.

**Transportation and Communications**

Singapore's transportation systems, including a modern subway, are excellent. Taxis are the best means for visitors to get around the city, and are convenient and inexpensive. Traffic congestion is not a major problem.

Telecommunications also are excellent and Fax machines are in wide use. International direct dialing is available throughout the city. The postal service is excellent and international courier services are widely available.

**Special Considerations**

Like most Asian societies, Singapore's society is hierarchical in comparison to that of the United States. Accordingly, Americans should pay close attention to the positions Singaporeans hold in their organizations and community, and make a point of deferring to persons in positions of importance.

Singapore's tight government controls provide a number of benefits, both substantive and tangential, to foreign business people. Intellectual property protection is good, there is virtually no corruption, and the bureaucracy is reasonably efficient.

Because of the scarcity of land and high import duties on automobiles (to help control traffic congestion), affluent Singaporeans often do not buy single family homes and expensive cars. Consequently, they tend to have more discretionary income than their economic peers elsewhere. This is one of a number of factors influencing a strong and growing consumer market in Singapore.

If you are discussing a prospective relationship with ethnic Malay Singaporeans, consult the Malaysia section of this guide for information on dealing with Malays.

**ENTRY REQUIREMENTS**

Americans need a passport, sufficient funds for the stay, and a ticket and documents for onward travel. No visa is required for business consultations except for stays in excess of 14 days.

**MONEY**

The unit of currency is the Singapore dollar, signified by the symbol S$. Cash is easily obtained at banks and hotels and, except at night, at currency exchanges at the airport upon arrival. Major credit cards are accepted throughout Singapore except at smaller shops. International travelers checks are accepted at banks and hotels and some of the larger establishments that cater to visitors.

One U.S. dollar is equal to about S$1.60.

**TIPPING**

You do not need to tip in Singapore. Tipping is officially discouraged. Restaurants and hotels, however, will add a ten percent service charge to your bill. If the services of a maid or driver have been especially thoughtful and personal, express your appreciation when you depart Singapore with a small gift such as candy.

**MAJOR HOLIDAYS**

| | |
|---|---|
| New Year's Day | January 1 |
| Chinese New Year | January/February* |
| Good Friday | Friday before Easter* |
| Hari Raya Puasa | April* |

* Date varies

|                 |                    |
|-----------------|--------------------|
| Labor Day       | May 1              |
| Vesak Day       | May 28             |
| Hari Raya Haji  | July*              |
| National Day    | August 9           |
| Deepavali       | October/November*  |
| Christmas Day   | December 25        |

**USEFUL PHRASES**

| English          | Mandarin*      | Phonetic Pronunciation |
|------------------|----------------|------------------------|
| Hello            | Ni hao         | Knee how               |
| Good morning     | Zao shang hao  | Tzaow shang how        |
| Good evening     | Wan shang hao  | Wahn shang how         |
| Good night       | Wan an         | Wahn ahn               |
| Good-bye         | Zai jian       | Dzye jee-en            |
| Yes              | Dui            | Doo-ee                 |
| No               | Bu dui         | Boo doo-ee             |
| Please           | Qing           | Ching                  |
| How much?        | Duo shao       | Doo-oh shah-oh         |
| Thank you        | Xie xie        | Shee-yeh shee-yeh      |
| You're welcome   | Bu xie         | Boo shee-yeh           |
| Cheers           | Gan bei        | Kahm pie               |
| I don't understand | Wo bu dong   | Wah boo dong           |

**USEFUL SINGAPORE CONTACTS**

Singapore Trade Development Board
1 Maritime Square #10-40
World Trade Centre
Telok Blangah Road
Singapore 0409
TELEPHONE: 65**/271-9388
FAX: 65-274-0770

Singapore Trade Development Board
Los Angeles World Trade Center
350 Figueroa Street
Los Angeles, CA 90071
TELEPHONE: 213/617-7358
FAX: 213/617-7367

Singapore Trade Development Board
745 Fifth Avenue
New York, NY 10151
TELEPHONE: 212/421-2207
FAX: 212/888-2897

Singapore Trade Development Board
Embassy of the Republic of Singapore
1824 R Street, N.W.
Washington, DC 20009-1691
TELEPHONE: 202/667-7555
FAX: 202/265-7915

---

* See the Hong Kong section of this guide for Cantonese and the Malaysia section for Bahasa Malaysia
** Singapore's country code

Singapore Economic Development Board
250 North Bridge Road #24-00
Raffles City Tower
Singapore 0617
TELEPHONE: 65-336-2288
FAX: 65-339-6077

Singapore Economic Development Board
55 Wheeler Street
Cambridge, MA 02138
TELEPHONE: 617/497-9392
FAX: 617/491-6150

Singapore Economic Development Board
Illinois Center Two
233 North Michigan Avenue
Chicago, IL 60601
TELEPHONE: 312/644-3730
FAX: 312/644-4481

Singapore Economic Development Board
Park Central VII
12750 Merit Drive
Dallas, TX 75251
TELEPHONE: 214/450-4540
FAX: 214/450-4543

Singapore Economic Development Board
2049 Century Park East
Los Angeles, CA 90067
TELEPHONE: 213/553-0199
FAX: 213/557-1044

Singapore Economic Development Board
55 East 59th Street
New York, NY 10022
TELEPHONE: 212/421-2200
FAX: 212/421-2206

Singapore Economic Development Board
210 Twin Dolphin Drive
Redwood City, CA 94065
TELEPHONE: 415/591-9102
FAX: 415/591-1328

Singapore Economic Development Board
1015 18th Street, N.W.
Washington, DC 20036
TELEPHONE: 202/223-2571
FAX: 202/223-2572

U.S. Embassy
Commercial Section
One Colombo Court #05-12
Singapore 0617
TELEPHONE: 65-338-9722
FAX: 65-338-5010

American Business Council
1 Scotts Road #16-07
Shaw Centre
Singapore 0922
TELEPHONE: 65-235-0077
FAX: 65-732-5917

Singapore International Chamber of Commerce
50 Raffles Place #03-02
Shell Tower
Singapore 0104
TELEPHONE: 65-224-1255
FAX: 65-224-2785

# COUNTRY PROFILE: SOUTH KOREA

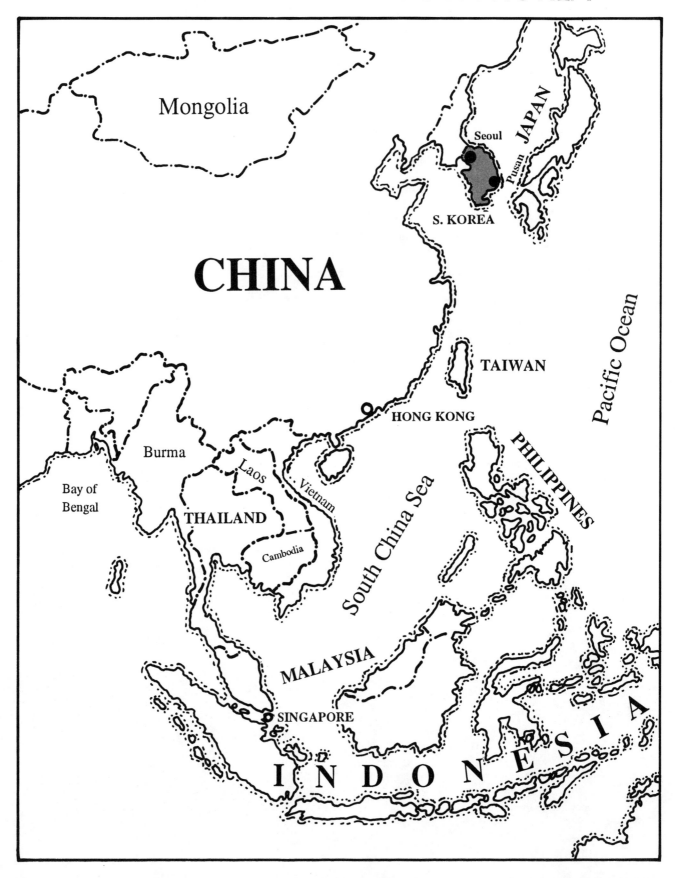

## EAST MEETS WEST IN THE KIMCHIBURGER

"The way to succeed in Asia is to roll up your sleeves and become a part of the country's way of life—in the neighborhoods and with localized products," says Jay Tunney, President of Uncle Joe's Hamburgers and Ice Cream, Seoul, South Korea.

Tunney fought for his success with a tenacity inherited from his famous father, Gene Tunney, who was heavyweight boxing champion of the world in the 1920s.

Tunney went to South Korea in late 1987 with a franchise for Hobson's California ice cream and a plan to open a string of ice cream parlors. He opened the first store in Seoul's popular Itaewon district shortly before the 1988 Summer Olympics, but he had to close it after about a year. "Koreans just weren't ready for ice cream parlors," says Tunney. "Their eating habits don't include popping out for a splurge on ice cream like youngsters might do in other markets." So he concentrated on supplying ice cream to hotels and bakery chains while he sought a way back into the retail mainstream.

Finally, on a side street in the heart of Seoul, Tunney happened across a hole-in-the-wall hamburger store called "Uncle Joe's." It served a terrific hamburger and had something of a cult following among local office workers, foreign business people, and diplomats. Before long, Tunney had bought out Uncle Joe's from its owner, who was ready to retire, and the foundations for today's Uncle Joe's chain began forming. After the new Uncle Joe's was well established, Tunney began marketing franchises.

One of the most popular items on an Uncle Joe's menu is Tunney's own invention, the "kimchiburger," a combination of kimchi (a spicy Korean cabbage dish) and Tunney's special recipe hamburger. Ice cream sells well too, as a complement to Uncle Joe's hamburgers and other fast food items.

Today there are 47 Uncle Joe's in South Korea; 24 in Seoul and 23 scattered throughout the country. There is even one as far removed as Cheju-do, the country's southernmost island. Tunney's company owns and operates the first showcase store in downtown Seoul and franchises the rest. Aggregate annual sales of all the Uncle Joe's stores are over $6 million.

Tunney runs his business, with the help of 35 employees, from a cramped office in the northern part of Seoul. In addition to managing the Uncle Joe's chain, the company supplies ice cream to nearly all the country's hotels and many of its major restaurants.

In seeking Uncle Joe's franchisees, Tunney avoids "Main Street." Instead, he looks for Korean business people in populous, local neighborhoods who are looking for a change in their line of business and can afford to rent premises to start up a store. Tunney sells the franchise, provides training and store interior decoration services, and supplies equipment, hamburger patties, buns, ice cream, and paper products; virtually all the store items except for a few perishables. Hamburger beef and ice cream flavorings are imported from the United States.

According to Tunney, Americans who are thinking about doing business in South Korea should plan on plenty of frustrations in dealing with Korean laws and bureaucracy. "You need creative tenacity," he says. "If a door is closed, find a window or take another route."

"Once you establish your credibility and 'worthiness,' however," adds

Tunney, "everything goes pretty well. Koreans are fiercely patriotic, but they are fair to Americans. As employees, they couldn't be better. They're zealous, hard working, honest, and loyal."

## SOUTH KOREA: ECONOMIC BACKGROUND

For most Americans, the words South Korea conjure up memories of the Korean War or the movie and television series M*A*S*H. South Korea is not as familiar to Americans as many other Asian countries. Fewer Koreans have emigrated to the United States than Chinese or Filipinos. South Korean products are not as prevalent in American markets as those from Japan. But times are changing.

Today Americans are seeing more and more products with South Korean brand names like Samsung, Goldstar, and Hyundai. If they look even more closely, they will see "Made in Korea" labels on many other products with international brand names; e.g., IBM personal computer monitors and Reebok sneakers. If they are involved in heavy industry, they are well aware of South Korea's leadership in shipbuilding and in construction projects around the world.

South Korea has come a very long way in a short time. It is as if the country finally has been given a chance to demonstrate its capabilities. The Korean Peninsula, with China to the west, Japan to the east, and the Russia to the north, was occupied or invaded by one or the other of its neighbors for much of its history. Korea was "the meat in the sandwich" for these contending powers. Japan annexed Korea outright in 1910. Following World War II, the United States and the Soviet Union occupied Korea, dividing it at the 38th parallel into South Korea (the Republic of Korea) and North Korea (the People's Republic of Korea). In 1950, Soviet ambitions in the region led to the invasion of South Korea by North Korea and to the three year Korean War (1950-1953).

South Korea came into its own after the Korean War. While the 1950s were marked by political upheaval, the 1960s and 1970s saw growing stability and economic improvement. Then, in the 1980s, South Korea's economy boomed. Growth rates in 1986, 1987, and 1988 exceeded 12 percent. And growth continues.

In size, South Korea's land area is about equal to the state of Indiana's. Its population, at 43 million, is far larger than that of any American state. (California, with 30 million people, is the most heavily-populated U.S. state.)

Koreans, believed to have migrated originally from central Asia, are ethnically homogeneous and different in many ways from other Asians. Their language is different. They are also more emotional, and their quick temper and boisterous nature lead many to call them "the Irish of the East." Occasional student riots and labor unrest in South Korea are periodic reminders of this national characteristic.

The economic success of South Korea can be credited to two principal factors: the hard work and dedication of its people, and the close collaboration of business and government.

South Koreans work long and hard. Industrial workers average 56 hours on the job during a six-day work week, the highest average in the world. Children go to school six days a week 240 days a year, compared with children in the United States who go five days a week 180 days a year. Vacations for South Koreans of all ages are infrequent and short.

Business and government in South Korea are close partners. During the 1960s, President Park Chung Hee laid the foundations of this partnership by setting up large, government-owned corporations to develop key segments of the economy. These corporations, called *chaebols*, received the full financial and planning support of the government, and they thrived. Gradually they were turned over to private, family-led ownership, but their close relationships with the government continue. The government coordinates their activities and dictates in large part the industries in which each may participate. Today, large *chaebols* like Samsung, Hyundai, Daewoo, and Lucky-Goldstar tend to dominate business in South Korea.

South Korea's economy is largely export-driven, with manufactured goods constituting over 90 percent of its export volume. Its electronics industry has had the highest rates of growth in recent years. The country has limited natural resources, however, and must import many commodities for manufacturing. It also is energy-dependent, with only 22 percent of its energy needs produced domestically.

Like many developing countries, South Korea has a history of trade protection. It is slowly liberalizing trade, lowering barriers in response to pressure from the United States and other trading partners. On the political side, and with an eye to economic implications, the government has taken a number of steps to improve relations with China, Japan, and North Korea. The reunification of the Korean Peninsula is a primary political objective.

For American exporters of consumer products and services, South Korea is a heady mixture of challenge and opportunity. With a 1991 income per capita of about $6,250 and a rapidly growing economy, South Korea has all the earmarks of an expanding consumer market. However, in their patriotic and single-minded quest for economic superiority, South Koreans often shun imported products and conserve or invest much of their discretionary income.

For American exporters in the industrial sector, South Korea offers much promise. The country's rapid economic growth will produce substantial markets for the products, services, and new technologies needed to sustain its expanding manufacturing base.

## NEAR-TERM OUTLOOK

South Korea's economic growth will remain at about seven percent in 1993. Growth in consumer demand will be moderate, about seven percent. Imports will grow by eight percent and exports by twelve percent. Inflation, which was ten percent in 1991, should decline to an estimated seven percent in 1993.

Near-term moderation in South Korea's economic growth is due in part to a slowdown in the construction boom (in housing and industrial capacity) that prevailed in recent years. Stronger growth will emerge in 1994 as a result of improved industrial productivity and competitiveness. Consumer spending also should expand.

During 1993, the government and private industry will spend heavily on various environmental and pollution control projects, responding to a new awareness and long neglect. In addition, the government will continue work on numerous infrastructure projects, including a high-speed rail link between Seoul and Pusan and a new international airport near Seoul.

**LANGUAGE**

Korean is the official language of South Korea. Although Korean has many Chinese words and its grammar is similar to Japanese, it is a distinct language. Written Korean, in contrast to the Chinese ideographic system, employs a phonetic alphabet with relatively few characters. This unique phonetic system helps account for South Korea's having a high literacy rate of about 97 percent.

English is understood and spoken only to a limited extent in South Korea, although there are many in the senior ranks of business and government who speak and write English.

**RELIGION**

About 40 percent of the South Korean population is Buddhist, and about 40 percent is Christian (mostly Protestant). Other religions, including Islam and Taoism, are also followed by parts of the population. In addition, there is an undercurrent of native shamanism in the religious beliefs of many Koreans.

**VITAL ECONOMIC STATISTICS (1991 Estimates)**

| | |
|---|---|
| Population: | 42.9 million |
| Gross Domestic Product | US$ 270.3 billion |
| Income Per Capita | US$ 6,247 |
| Annual Growth Rate | 8.4 percent |
| Total Imports | US$ 75 billion |
| Total Exports | US$ 70.5 billion |
| U.S. Share of Manufactured Imports | 27.5 percent |
| U.S. Share of Total Exports | 28.1 percent |

**Top Five Imports From U.S.**

Non-electrical/electronics machinery and mechanical appliances
Electrical/electronics machinery and equipment
Cereals
Organic chemicals
Aircraft and aircraft parts

**Top Five Exports To U.S.**

Electrical/electronics machinery and equipment
Non-electrical/electronics machinery and mechanical appliances
Footwear
Articles of leather, travel goods
Apparel

**Top Three Foreign Investors**

U.S.
Japan
Germany

**Top Three Trading Partners**

U.S.
Japan
Germany

**BEST EXPORT OPPORTUNITIES FOR AMERICAN FIRMS***

**Electronics Industry Production and Test Equipment**

Advanced digital multimeters, oscilloscope equipment and parts, galvanometers

---

* U.S. Chamber of Commerce 1992 Rankings

| | |
|---|---|
| **Electronic Components** | Integrated circuits, parts of magnetic heads, prepared recording media |
| **Computers and Peripherals** | Engineering workstations, disk storage devices, printing devices |
| **Pollution Control Equipment** | Air and water pollution control equipment |
| **Automotive Parts and Service Equipment** | Automotive motors (for power windows, fuel, antennas, wipers), fan clutch, brake hose and electrical control unit, electrical equipment for testing motors |
| **CAD/CAM/CAE/CIM** | (Computer Assisted Design/Manufacturing/Engineering; Computer Integrated Manufacturing) MCAD, EDA (ECAD), AEC |
| **Building Products** | Wood products, tubes and pipes |
| **Computer Software and Services** | Utility software, applications software for microcomputers (database, spread sheets, graphics, DTP, communications, LAN packs) |
| **Process Controls—Industrial** | Programmable logic controller, process controls for pulp and paper industry |
| **Pumps, Valves, and Compressors** | Hydraulic fluid power pumps, industrial pumps |
| **Telecommunications Equipment** | Telephone sets, teleprinters, fax equipment, key telephones and private branch exchanges |
| **Telecommunications Services** | Mobile telecommunications services, cellular phone services, paging services, value-added network (VAN) services, communications processing VAN, information processing VAN, database VAN, domestic and international telephone services, international video transmission and broadcast services, data services |
| **Non-Computer Business Equipment** | Bar code systems, banking terminals |
| **Sporting Goods** | Golf equipment, bowling equipment |
| **Household Consumer Goods** | Cook ware, grinders, mixers, coffee makers |
| **Medical Equipment** | Cardiological equipment, implantable pacemakers |
| **Laboratory and Scientific Equipment** | Calorimeters, pH meters, and viscometers, frequency measuring apparatus, faults/cracks detectors, instruments |
| **Food Processing and Packaging Equipment** | Filling and sealing packaging machines, automatic wrapping machines, bakery machinery, heating/cooling plant and machinery |

| | |
|---|---|
| **Advertising Services** | |
| **Travel and Tourist Services** | Business, pleasure, employment travel services, VFR (visual flight rules) |
| **Welding Equipment** | Computerized special welding systems, plasma welding equipment, laser welding equipment |
| **Machine Tools and Metalworking Equipment** | CNC machine tools, lathes |
| **Railroad Equipment** | Rolling stock equipment, traffic control equipment |
| **Avionics and Ground Support Equipment** | Non-directional beacons, tactical omni-range, instrumental landing systems, test equipment |
| **Aviation/Helicopter Services** | |
| **Cosmetics and Toiletries** | Cosmetics |
| **Drugs and Pharmaceuticals** | Antibiotics, diagnostic reagents |
| **Franchising Services** | Fast food stores, convenience stores |
| **Aircraft and Parts** | Airplanes and helicopters, aircraft engines and parts |
| **Printing and Graphic Arts Equipment** | Sheet printing presses, rotary printing presses, phototypesetting machines, printing and binding machines |
| **Electric Power Systems** | Thermal power projects, electric generating equipment |
| **Industrial Chemicals** | Specialty chemicals |
| **Marine Fisheries** | Adjacent waters fisheries, deep-sea fisheries, aquaculture inland waters fisheries, inland water fisheries |
| **Pulp and Paper Processing Equipment** | |
| **Processed Foods** | Alcoholic beverages, fast foods, other processed foods |
| **Jewelry** | Diamond jewelry |
| **Architectural/Construction/ Engineering Services** | Airport design, high speed rail projects, nuclear power projects |
| **Yarns** | Synthetic filaments, staple fibers |

**Water Resources Equipment**   Water quality test equipment, measuring equipment

## BUSINESS PRACTICES

### Meetings

Americans should not try to arrange meetings directly with Koreans whom they do not already know. They should ask a colleague, a South Korean government office, a bank or consultant to arrange the meetings through an exchange of correspondence.

It is sometimes difficult to make specific meeting arrangements prior to your arrival in South Korea, but appointments will usually fall into place once it is known that you are in the country.

Meetings in Korea are reasonably formal affairs. As is virtually always the case in Asia, however, business discussions should be preceded by social conversation.

If your meetings involve negotiations, expect long hours and intense discussions. Koreans are known to be tough, sometimes emotional, negotiators. In contrast to other Asians, they tend to be direct and aggressive.

Punctuality and careful preparation are important for meetings in South Korea. Business points will be discussed in great detail, so Americans should allow plenty of time to complete a business transaction.

Business discussions are often held in restaurants over breakfast, lunch, or dinner.

### Business Hours

Business office hours are normally six days a week, Monday through Friday, from 9 a.m. to 6 p.m., and Saturday from 9 a.m. to 1 p.m. A lunch hour is taken on weekdays from about 12:30 p.m. to 1:30 p.m.

### Greetings

Shaking hands is the usual greeting for men and women in business settings in South Korea. This often is also combined with a slight bow. An American man, however, should shake hands with a Korean woman only if she extends her hand first. American business women should be the first to extend their hands to Korean men and women.

### Business Cards

The exchange of business cards on the occasion of a first meeting is an important practice in South Korea. Cards should be presented and received with both hands. Take a moment to read each card you receive, showing some interest and appreciation. Do not immediately shove the card into your pocket.

Americans should have their cards printed in Korean on one side.

### Names and Titles

In South Korea, it is more of a problem for Americans to keep people straight than names straight. This is because so many Koreans are named Park, Kim, Lee (roughly estimated to be about half the population), or one of several other common names.

South Koreans normally have three names. The first is the family name, the next two are a clan name and a given name (or vice versa). Outside their immediate families, they are always addressed by their family name, often followed by the honorific *sôngsaengnim* (song-sang-nim), which means "respected person," or by *sôngsaengnim* alone. Titles also are normally used, as in "Manager Kim" or "Engineer Park." Americans should use these forms of address or use the family name with "Mr.," "Mrs.," "Miss," or "Dr.," as appropriate. ("Ms." is seldom used in South Korea.) They should not try to use a Korean's given name.

A South Korean's family name does not always appear first, however. Those who are in frequent contact with the international business community sometimes place their family names last, Western style.

**Clothing**   South Koreans dress conservatively and well. American business men visiting South Korea should wear suits and ties, preferably with a plain white shirt. Suits and ties of dark or subdued colors are best. Business women should wear suits or dresses. Pants are not appropriate for women in business settings but are acceptable for evening and informal wear.

**Gifts and Entertainment**   Gift-giving is common in South Korea, but not normally on first meeting. You may let your host lead the way. When the circumstances indicate that a gift is appropriate (for example, after the host presents you with a gift or when you are entertained by him), you should reciprocate either with a gift (one of good quality) or by hosting a luncheon or dinner. Good gifts in South Korea are pens or leather items with your organization's logo, classical music cassette tapes, liquor (scotch or cognac are popular), and items from your area of the United States.

Gifts are presented and received with both hands, and are not normally opened in the presence of the giver.

Koreans often entertain in bars, restaurants, and private clubs, frequently with hostesses taking part in the festivities. In keeping with their nature, they do so with gusto. It is here that Americans' tolerance of liquor will be tested. It is the custom that each person at the table play host to the guest of honor by pouring a drink for the guest, and it is expected that the guest will promptly down each. There is no easy way out for men (women are not expected to keep up), but possible precautions on these occasions are to consume plenty of rice, avoid strong drinks and large glasses, or claim total abstinence.

South Koreans seldom entertain in their homes. However, if they do, good gifts for Americans to take to the host and hostess are flowers, a cake, a fruit basket, liquor, or champagne, all of which can be obtained locally.

**Conversation**   In keeping with the collectivist culture of South Korea, the best topics of conversation are those relating to families and organizations. Americans will be asked about their age, marital status, their siblings, and their positions in their organizations. Koreans do not intend to pry; these questions merely help them to understand where one fits in the hierarchies and relationships of these all-important groups. Americans may ask similar questions.

Topics that compliment South Korea, such as its economic gains, also are good. Political and religious topics, and questions about student and labor unrest, should be avoided. In general, Americans should avoid being critical, abrupt or judgmental in any negative way.

**Hotels**   There are many fine hotels in South Korean cities. They feature excellent facilities, service, and dining. They also serve as meeting and entertainment centers for visiting and local business people. Their business is brisk, so one should make reservations well in advance.

**Exercise**   A number of hotels in South Korea have excellent exercise facilities for their guests. If your hotel has none, try those of another hotel since some are open to the public.

Jogging is excellent in parks and sometimes on hotel grounds. In Seoul, it is enjoyable to jog on the historic and picturesque palace grounds of Ch'angdokkung, Kyongbokkung, and Toksukung.

Standard athletic wear is acceptable attire for men and women, except that women should wear pants rather than shorts.

**Transportation and Communications**   There is much traffic congestion in South Korean cities, especially in Seoul. Visitors should allow extra time to get where they are going. Taxis normally are the best means for visitors to get around a city, but it is often difficult to hail one on the street. In Seoul, it is sometimes better to walk or ride the (modern) subway. In some cases, a South Korean company will arrange a car and driver to transport a visitor to and from a meeting.

Telecommunications are excellent in South Korea. Fax machines are in wide use. International direct dialing is available throughout the country and international courier services also are widely available.

**Special Considerations**   Age is venerated in South Korea, so it is important to show respect toward older people regardless of their position in an organization or the circumstances in which you meet them.

Women are accorded high respect in their roles of mothers and wives, but they seldom are found in the upper echelons of business or government. South Korea is a highly male oriented society. It is sometimes disconcerting to American business women to find that their lower-ranking male associates are paid greater attention by Koreans than they are. This is largely unconscious behavior, however, with no offense intended. Koreans readily defer to persons of authority, whether they be male or female.

Although Korean women are not influential in business and government, they exert considerable influence over families' buying decisions. Therefore, exporters of American products and services often need to direct their marketing efforts more to Korean women than to Korean men.

It takes time and effort to develop good relations with Koreans. They are basically distrustful of foreigners, probably because of centuries of their mistreatment at the hands of others who have occupied their lands. Feelings are especially bitter toward the Japanese for atrocities committed during World War II. Attitudes toward Americans are generally good among Korean business people, but many students and liberals harbor resentment toward the United States based on the long U.S. military presence in South Korea.

Just as Koreans tend to be more emotional and aggressive than most Asians, they also tend to be more individualistic. They are more entrepreneurial and they take more risks. They tend to be more time-conscious and sensitive to deadlines and schedules than many of their

Asian counterparts. They also value more highly various personal factors such as titles and executive perks. Americans should keep these considerations in mind when negotiating with Koreans.

Intellectual property rights are protected in South Korea with patent and copyright laws, but law enforcement lags, and there is no trade secret protection. Also, although trade barriers are easing, many still exist in the form of tariffs and licensing requirements. Among problems that American exporters face is the practical inability of South Korean businesses to import on credit.

## ENTRY REQUIREMENTS

Americans on business need a passport, a notarized letter of guarantee from their company, a visa, sufficient funds for the stay, and a ticket and documents for onward travel.

## MONEY

South Korea's unit of currency is the *won*, indicated by the symbol KW. Cash is easily obtained at banks and hotels and, except at night, at currency exchanges at the airport upon arrival. Major credit cards are accepted in hotels and larger shops and restaurants. International travelers checks are normally accepted only at banks and hotels.

One U.S. dollar is equal to about KW780.

## TIPPING

Tipping normally is not expected in South Korea. However, porters are normally tipped 100 *won* per bag. Taxi drivers are not normally tipped unless they help with luggage, at which time a tip of about 700 *won* is appreciated. Restaurants and hotels will add a service charge of ten percent.

## MAJOR HOLIDAYS

| | |
|---|---|
| New Year's Day | January 1 |
| New Year's holiday | January 2 |
| Independence Movement Day | March 1 |
| Labor Day | March 10 |
| Arbor Day | April 5 |
| Buddha's Birthday | May* |
| Children's Day | May 5 |
| Memorial Day | June 6 |
| Constitution Day | July 17 |
| Liberation Day | August 15 |
| Thanksgiving (two days) | September/October* |
| Armed Forces Day | October 1 |
| National Foundation Day | October 3 |
| Hangul Day | October 9 |
| Christmas Day | December 25 |

## USEFUL PHRASES

| English | Korean | Phonetic Pronunciation |
|---|---|---|
| Hello | Yôboseyo | Yah-bo-say-oh |
| Good morning | Annyong hashimnika | Ahn-yohng hah-ship-nee-kah |
| Good evening | (same) | (same) |
| Good night | (same) | (same) |
| Good-bye | Annyonghee kaseyo | Ahn-yohng-hee kah-say-o |
| Yes | Ne | Neh |

---

\* Date varies according to lunar calendar

| English | Korean | Phonetic Pronunciation |
|---------|--------|------------------------|
| No | Aniyo | Ah-nee-yo |
| Please | Chom | Chohm |
| How much? | Ollma imnika? | Ole-mah im-nee-kah? |
| Thank you | Kamsa hamnida | Kahm-sah hahm-nee-dah |
| You're welcome | Ch'onmaneyo | Chon-mahn-ay-yo |
| Cheers | Kônbae | Kohn-bai |
| I don't understand | Chal morûgetsumnida | Chahl mor-oo-get-soom-nee-dah |

## USEFUL SOUTH KOREA CONTACTS

Korean Trade Promotion Corporation
159, Samsung-dong, Kangnam-gu
Trade Center Box 123
Seoul, Republic of Korea
TELEPHONE: 82*/2-551-4181
FAX: 82-2-551-4477

Korea Trade Promotion Corporation
111 East Wacker Drive
Chicago, IL 60601
TELEPHONE: 312/644-4323
FAX: 312/644-4879

Korea Trade Promotion Corporation
(Exhibition Center)
1000 Tower Lane
Bensenville, IL 60106
TELEPHONE: 708/350-0102
FAX: 708/350-0747

Korea Trade Promotion Corporation
P.O. Box 58023
Dallas, TX 75258-0023
TELEPHONE: 214/748-9341
FAX: 214/748-4630

Korea Trade Promotion Corporation
4801 Wilshire Boulevard
Los Angeles, CA 90010
TELEPHONE: 213/954-9500
FAX: 213954-1707

Korea Trade Promotion Corporation
One Biscayne Tower
Miami, FL 33131
TELEPHONE: 305/374-4648
FAX: 305/375-9332

Korea Trade Promotion Corporation
460 Park Avenue
New York, NY 10022
TELEPHONE: 212/826-0900
FAX: 212/888-4930

* South Korea's country code

Korea Trade Promotion Corporation
1129 20th Street
Washington, DC 20036
TELEPHONE: 202/857-7919
FAX: 202/857-7923

Korea Foreign Trade Association
Korea World Trade Center
159-1, Samsung-dong, Kangnam-gu
Seoul, Republic of Korea
TELEPHONE: 82-2-551-5114
FAX: 82-2-551-5100

Association of Foreign Trading Agents of Korea
45-20, Youido-dong, Yongdungpo-gu
Seoul, Republic of Korea
TELEPHONE: 82-2-782-4411
FAX: 82-2-785-4373

Korea Chamber of Commerce and Industry
45, Namdaemun-no, Chung-ku, CPOB 25
Seoul, Republic of Korea
TELEPHONE: 82-2-757-0757
FAX: 82-2-757-9475

U.S. Embassy
Commercial Section
82, Sejong-Ro, Chongro-ku
Seoul, Republic of Korea
TELEPHONE: 82-2-732-2601
FAX: 82-2-738-8845

American Chamber of Commerce in Korea
Westin Chosun Hotel
87, Sogong-dong, Chung-gu
Seoul, Republic of Korea
TELEPHONE: 82-2-753-6471
FAX: 82-2-755-6577

Korea Economic Institute of America
1101 Vermont Avenue, N.W.
Washington, DC 20005-0690
TELEPHONE: 202/371-0690
FAX: 202/371-0692

# COUNTRY PROFILE: TAIWAN

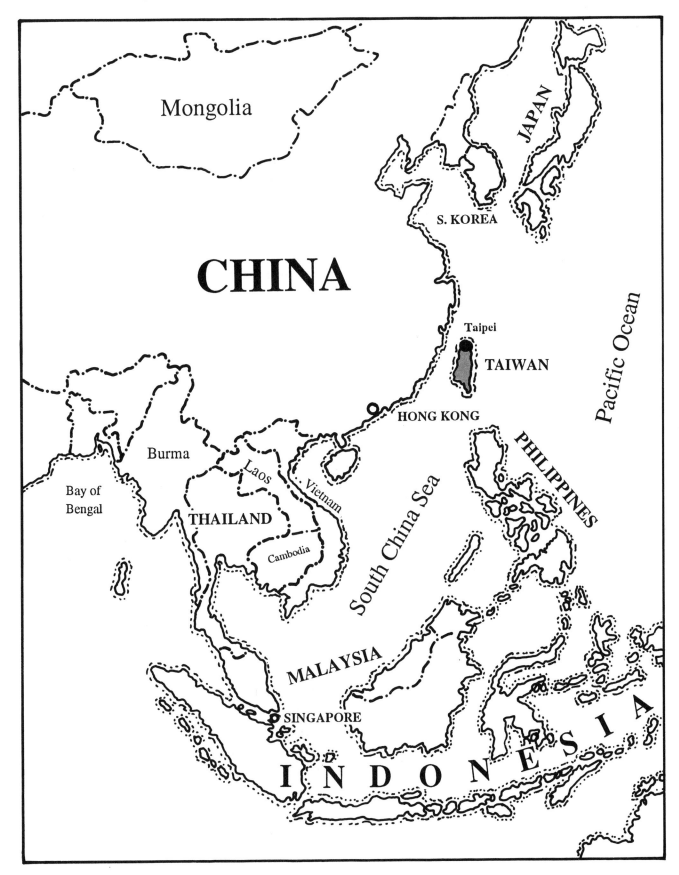

## QUALITY PAYS IN TAIPEI

"Our experience in Asia is that quality is the key to success," says Marc Finkelstein, President of Hughes-Treitler Manufacturing Corporation of Garden City, New York.

Finkelstein ought to know. Hughes-Treitler has forged a solid reputation for quality products during its 45 years as a supplier of manufactured components for the aircraft and aerospace industries. Originally a supplier of fabricated "black boxes" that hold aircraft electronics, Hughes-Treitler began in 1970 to develop a line of heat exchanger and cooling products for aircraft and ground equipment. They pioneered a process called aluminum vacuum brazing which enabled them to produce heat exchangers of greater capacity and reliability. Today they are the largest aluminum vacuum brazed heat exchanger manufacturer in the aerospace industry, and the only private one. (Other heat exchanger manufacturers are divisions of public companies.)

The company's success has not gone unrecognized. It received Vendor of the Year Awards from the U.S. Small Business Administration in 1977 and again in 1983.

Hughes-Treitler (no relation to Hughes Aircraft) employs 200 people at its 75,000 square foot manufacturing facility on Long Island. With annual sales in excess of $20 million, its business mix is now about 60 percent commercial and 40 percent military. Its products are incorporated in General Electric and Pratt & Whitney aircraft engines, on Boeing and Airbus planes, and on military aircraft manufactured in Sweden, Italy, and Taiwan.

Hughes-Treitler started selling its products to Taiwan four years ago and has begun selling into Japan. "Asia is our most rapidly expanding market," says Finkelstein. In Taiwan, the company supplies its heat exchangers for manufacture of the IDF military fighter, a plane similar to the United States' F-16.

The company got its first Taiwan contract by bidding for it. Subsequently, more business has been obtained on the basis of negotiated agreements. So far, all of the Taiwan business is with the Chung Shan Institute of Science and Technology, Taiwan's large, government-owned aerospace agency.

"The executives and engineers of Chung Shan's Defense Procurement Division are very professional and very hard working," says Finkelstein. "Our relations are quite formal and entirely above board. We don't do much socializing with them, in part because they're government people."

In dealing with the Taiwanese, according to Finkelstein, diligence is extremely important. "You have to spend much more time in preparing, presenting, and explaining your proposals than if you were dealing with an American firm," he says. "They pay careful attention to the details, and you have to have plenty of patience."

"The good part," says Finkelstein, "is that once your proposals are accepted everything goes very smoothly. There are no glitches. Nothing has been forgotten. There are no problems."

"And best of all," adds Finkelstein, "the Taiwanese are willing to pay for quality."

## TAIWAN: ECONOMIC BACKGROUND

For a small country, Taiwan (the Republic of China) has plenty of chutzpah. And it thinks BIG.

A country about the size of Massachusetts and Connecticut combined, Taiwan is less than one half of one percent of the size of mainland China (the People's Republic of China) and has less than two percent of its population. Yet when Chiang Kai-shek's Nationalist Party lost China's civil war to Mao Zedong's Communist Party in 1949 and set up its government on Taiwan, it nonetheless claimed to be the true government of all of China and vowed to return to power someday. It still maintains that position, even though the United States and other Western nations withdrew political support of Taiwan in favor of China during the 1970s.

There is nothing to suggest that Taiwan will ever succeed in regaining power over mainland China. (However, there is much to suggest that the two will merge someday. China has never recognized Taiwan as an independent nation. Trade and investment between the two are steadily increasing, and the rhetoric on both sides is much less strident in recent years.) Nevertheless, Taiwan's proportional economic strength is formidable. This small nation, until 1950 largely an agrarian backwater of mainland China, now has one of the strongest economies in Asia and is the world's thirteenth largest trading economy. Agriculture now accounts for only about five percent of Taiwan's gross national product, with manufacturing accounting for about 37 percent and services for about 54 percent.

Taiwan's economic growth was sparked by U.S. military aid during the Korean War (1950-1953). Its leaders soon moved the country swiftly toward an export-driven free enterprise economy. Large government-owned corporations were set up to develop strategic industries such as steel, petrochemicals, shipbuilding, and energy. New airports, highways, railways, seaports, and communications systems were built. Foreign investment was encouraged.

Despite the significant influence of Taiwan's large, government-owned corporations, the strength of the economy lies principally in its many small, entrepreneurial firms. In the manufacturing sector, fully 85 percent of Taiwan's factories employ fewer than 50 workers. The Taiwanese are especially proficient in product development, designing new products and bringing them to market faster than anywhere else in the world.

Recently the government has taken steps to encourage Taiwan businesses to move more rapidly into high technology, value-added activities, and to invest in production facilities in other countries (largely in Southeast Asia) where labor costs are lower. Steps have also been taken to privatize some of Taiwan's government-owned industries. Government-held stock has been sold in the China Steel Corporation and several public commercial banks. Other industries, including paper, chemicals, and construction, are targeted for privatization.

Continuing to think big, Taiwan approved a huge Six-Year Economic Development Plan in 1991 calling for $302 billion to be spent by the government and private industry on public works and industrial projects during 1991-1996. The plan contemplates substantial infrastructure improvements, anti-pollution projects, technology gains, energy diversification, and capital-intensive industrial developments. It also provides for various trade and financial liberalization measures designed to help the country achieve its economic targets.

Westerners once knew Taiwan as Formosa, the name given it in the 1600s by the Portuguese, who called it Ilha Formosa, "Beautiful Island." Its present name, Taiwan, means "Terraced Bay" in Chinese. As a result of its proximity to trade routes (it lies off the east coast of China, between Japan and the Philippines), Taiwan was occupied from time to time by the Dutch, the Spanish, and the French. In 1874 it was invaded by the Japanese and remained under Japanese control until the end of World War II when it was returned to Chinese rule.

Culturally, politically, and economically, Taiwan has remained predominantly Chinese throughout its history. Some 85 percent of its inhabitants are descendants of emigrants from mainland China's neighboring Fukien and Kwangtung provinces. The remainder of the population are "mainlanders" who arrived from various Chinese provinces since 1949.

Apart from its ethnic and cultural homogeneity, Taiwan is a nation of great diversity. There are high mountains and open seas. Half of the island is covered with forests. There are forestry and fishery industries. One-third of the land is arable, producing rice, wheat, corn, and other crops, and supporting livestock. Manufacturing now produces virtually everything from low tech garments to high tech computers, from household television sets to very large oceangoing freight and oil carriers.

Taipei, Taiwan's capital city and commercial heart, gives the business visitor the distinct impression that Taiwan will succeed in its economic ambitions. It is a lively, energetic city bursting with vitality. Its traffic jams and sprawling growth are characteristic of Taiwan's urgent quest for achievement.

Taiwan's plans for a broad expansion of its infrastructure and manufacturing base present many opportunities for American businesses. There also is an expanding consumer market in Taiwan, where 1991 per capita income, at $8,400, is the fourth highest in Asia.

## NEAR-TERM OUTLOOK

Taiwan's economy will be boosted during 1993 by economic recovery in the United States, its largest export market, and heavy spending on public works and industrial projects under its $302 billion Six-Year Economic Development Plan. The economy will grow by seven percent in 1993. Exports are projected to expand by ten percent and imports by eleven percent. Barring unanticipated adverse developments, the economy should do as well for at least several additional years.

Strong economic activity will put upward pressure on wage rates and the cost of building materials. Inflation will rise from four percent in 1992 to five percent in 1993. Consumer demand will rise by an estimated seven percent in 1993.

Public and private sector expenditures under the Six-Year Economic Development Plan will rise substantially during 1993, especially for engineering and construction services and capital equipment. The Plan encompasses 775 projects, including six mass rapid-transit systems, a new north-south highway, a high-speed railway, and a fourth nuclear power plant.

**LANGUAGE**

Mandarin is the official language of Taiwan and the language of instruction in schools. English is spoken as a second language by about 50 percent of the population, especially in business circles and among young people. It is taught to all students as their first foreign language, beginning in the seventh grade. Taiwanese, a southern Fukien dialect, also is widely spoken.

**RELIGION**

Buddhism and Taoism are the predominant religions of Taiwan. About 5 percent of the population is Christian, and a small minority is Muslim. There are temples and churches of various faiths throughout the country.

**VITAL ECONOMIC STATISTICS (1991 Estimates)**

| | |
|---|---|
| Population: | 20.4 million |
| Gross Domestic Product | US$ 168.6 billion |
| Income Per Capita | US$ 8,400 |
| Annual Growth Rate | 7 percent |
| Total Imports | US$ 60.8 billion |
| Total Exports | US$ 72.4 billion |
| U.S. Share of Manufactured Imports | 22.6 percent |
| U.S. Share of Total Exports | 30.1 percent |

**Top Five Imports From U.S.**

Electrical machinery and equipment and parts
Nuclear reactors, boilers, machinery and mechanical appliances, parts
Organic chemicals
Vehicles other than rail or tram rolling stock, and parts and accessories
Optical, photographic, cinematographic, measuring, checking precision, medical or surgical instruments and apparatus, parts and accessories

**Top Five Exports To U.S.**

Electrical machinery and equipment and parts
Nuclear reactors, boilers, machinery and mechanical appliances and parts
Footwear and gaiters, and parts
Furniture, household materials and appliances, prefabricated buildings
Toys, games, sporting goods, and accessories

**Top Three Foreign Investors**

Japan
U.S.
Hong Kong

**Top Three Trading Partners**

U.S.
Japan
Hong Kong

**BEST EXPORT OPPORTUNITIES FOR AMERICAN FIRMS***

**Pollution Control Equipment**

Waste water treatment, solid waste treatment

**Computers and Peripherals**

Large-scale computers, medium-scale computers, minicomputers, workstations

---

* U.S. Chamber of Commerce 1992 Rankings

| | |
|---|---|
| **Laboratory Scientific Instruments** | Analytical, electronic, medical, measuring instruments |
| **Electronics Industry Production and Test Equipment** | Semiconductor production equipment, electronic test equipment |
| **Process Controls—Industrial** | Electronic/electric instruments, process control computers and peripherals |
| **Medical Equipment** | Medical/surgical, electro-medical diagnostic and ophthalmic apparatus, orthopedic appliances, prostheses, hearing aids, pacemakers, mechanotherapy and respiratory appliances |
| **Telecommunications Equipment** | Telephone and telex/telegraph equipment |
| **Electric Power Systems** | Steam and other vapor generating boilers, AC generators |
| **Electronic Components** | Integrated circuits, PC boards |
| **Industrial Chemicals** | Ethylene, propylene, butadiene, benzene |
| **Plastic Materials and Resins** | Engineering plastics, synthetic resins |
| **Air-Conditioning and Refrigeration Equipment** | |
| **Automobiles and Light Trucks/Vans** | Sedans |
| **Household Consumer Goods** | Home appliances |
| **Processed Foods** | Beverages, grain mill products, frozen food, dairy products, bakery products, sugar confectionery, canned food |
| **CAD/CAM/CAE/CIM** | (Computer Assisted Design/Manufacturing/Engineering; Computer Integrated Manufacturing) CAD/CAM |
| **Lasers and Electro-Optics** | Optical electronic semiconductors, optical information products, optical testing and controlling instruments |
| **Cosmetics and Toiletries** | |
| **Aircraft and Parts** | Aircraft |
| **Travel and Tourist Services** | Inbound and outbound services |
| **Insurance Services** | Life insurance, property insurance |

| | |
|---|---|
| **Architectural/Construction/ Engineering Services** | |
| **Construction Equipment** | Construction and earth moving equipment, construction and materials handling equipment |
| **Drugs and Pharmaceuticals** | Medicaments, pharmaceuticals for malnutrition, antibiotics, vitamins |
| **Avionics and Ground Support Equipment** | Radar apparatus, aircraft ground support equipment, air terminal communications systems |
| **Chemical Production Machinery** | Steam and vapor generating boilers, heat exchangers |
| **Building Products** | Wood and plywood building products, plumbing and heating products, chemical/petrochemical building products |
| **Coal** | Bituminous coal |
| **Printing and Graphic Arts Equipment** | Offset printing machinery, phototype-setting and composing machines |
| **Automotive Parts and Service Equipment** | Automotive parts |
| **Marine Fisheries Products (Seafood)** | Fish fillets, frozen halibut, frozen cod, frozen fish roes, frozen crab, frozen lobster, frozen scallops |
| **Railroad Equipment** | Diesel-electric locomotives and parts, self-propelled railway or tramway coaches, vans and trucks, traffic control equipment |
| **Food Processing and Packaging Equipment** | |
| **Trucks, Trailers, and Buses** | Trucks |
| **Hotel and Restaurant Equipment** | Food preparation equipment, refrigeration equipment, food warming and serving products, cooking equipment |
| **Security and Safety Equipment** | Premises protection, communications equipment and cameras, fire protection/rescue equipment, commodity protection |
| **Information Services** | On-line databases |
| **Franchising Services** | Food retailing, educational products and services, laundry and dry cleaning services |
| **Textile Fabrics** | Special woven fabrics, tufted textile fabrics, lace, tapestries, trimmings, embroidery |

| | |
|---|---|
| **Wood Products** | Hardwood lumber, softwood lumber, veneer sheets, wood fiberboard, particle boards |

## BUSINESS PRACTICES

**Meetings**

Meetings should be arranged well in advance, as a courtesy and because the schedules of Taiwan business people normally are crowded. Americans who do not know the persons whom they want to meet should arrange meetings through an intermediary who knows both parties. This can be accomplished through a colleague, a Taiwan government office or business association, or a consultant. The intermediary will make the arrangements with an exchange of correspondence. Sometimes an intermediary can make appointments on short notice with a telephone call.

Americans should approach meetings with Taiwanese business people as serious, not casual, affairs. Punctuality, formality, and careful preparation are important in Taiwan. However, all business discussions should start with relaxed social conversation in order to develop good relations between the parties.

Business discussions are frequently conducted over lunch or dinner. Business breakfasts are uncommon in Taiwan (except in hotels) because few restaurants open before 10 a.m.

When meetings consist of extensive and intensive business negotiations, they may last for long hours over many days.

**Business Hours**

Offices are normally open six days a week, Monday through Friday from 8:30 a.m. to 5:30 p.m. and Saturday from 8:30 a.m. to noon. Lunch on weekdays normally is taken from noon to 1 p.m.

**Greetings**

A slight bow is the common greeting in Taiwan, except in business circles where most people—men and women—shake hands. American business men, however, should permit Taiwanese women to extend their hands first. To avoid confusion, American business women should extend their hands first to both men and women.

When meeting several people at once, higher-ranking and older persons should be greeted first.

**Business Cards**

Business cards should always be exchanged in Taiwan on first meeting. Cards should be presented with the right hand or with both hands, and the print should face the recipient.

It is advisable but not necessary to have your cards printed in Chinese on one side.

**Names and Titles**

The Taiwanese normally have three words in their names. The first, in keeping with Chinese tradition, is the family name. Americans always should address a Taiwan person by the family name together with the person's title (as in "Manager Lee" or "Vice President Wong") or with the appropriate honorific, "Mr.," "Mrs.," "Miss," or "Dr." (as in "Mr. Chen" or "Miss Huang"). "Ms." is seldom used in Taiwan. In formal settings, use a person's title instead of the honorific.

A Taiwanese woman normally retains her family name rather than taking the name of her husband.

Notwithstanding Chinese tradition, Taiwan business people who deal frequently with Westerners often place their family name last. If you are not sure which is the family name, it is best to consult an associate or to ask the person directly.

Americans should resist the impulse to "get on a first name basis" with a Taiwanese by using the person's given name, no matter how friendly a tone has been set for the business meetings and negotiations. This is not accepted practice in Taiwan (indeed, in most of Asia) and will tend to strain rather than improve the relationship.

### Clothing

Conservative Western-style clothing is the most appropriate attire for Taiwan: suits and ties of dark or subdued colors for men, skirts and blouses or dresses for women.

### Gifts and Entertainment

While gifts are appreciated by Taiwan business people they are not expected, especially on first meeting. In any event, gifts should not be lavish or overly personal. Good business gifts include pens and paperweights with the logo of your organization and items from your part of the United States such as photograph books or cassette tapes of your city's symphony orchestra. If a more expensive gift is warranted, a bottle of good quality scotch or cognac will be appreciated.

Gifts should be presented and received with both hands. An American receiving a gift should not open it in the presence of the giver. Similarly, Americans should not insist that their gift to a Taiwanese be opened immediately.

Items that should not be given: knives or letter openers (they suggest the cutting of relationships), clocks (associated with funerals), and handkerchiefs (signifying departure).

Hosting a luncheon or dinner for your Taiwan associates is always a good alternative to gift-giving. If the occasion is special, such as the commencement of a joint venture, a dinner together with a gift for the senior Taiwan official (who will accept on behalf of his contingent) is appropriate.

The Taiwanese occasionally entertain at home. If this occurs, good gifts for Americans to take to the host and hostess are flowers, a fruit basket, or a bottle of good quality scotch or cognac.

### Conversation

Topics of interest to Taiwan people tend to be more personal than Americans normally encounter. They will want to know many details of your family life and your work, including the nature and value of some of your possessions. Americans who are uncomfortable with this may choose simply not to remember.

The Taiwanese, for whom bargaining and trade is part of life, are also always interested in the price and value of things. Taiwan's excellent Chinese food and other national attributes also are good topics of conversation. Topics to avoid are those involving mainland China and other political issues.

**Hotels**   Taiwan has some excellent hotels. Because their occupancy rates are high, visitors should make reservations well in advance. In Taipei, if your appointments are in the business and financial districts, it is wise to select a hotel on the eastern side of the city in order to minimize problems with traffic congestion.

Taipei hotels feature especially fine service, and typically they have excellent facilities for business meetings and entertainment.

**Exercise**   Most Taipei hotels have good exercise facilities for their guests.

Jogging and walking are good forms of exercise in Taiwan if streets are not too congested or if a park is accessible. Another good activity is *tai chi*, the early morning ballet-like martial arts exercise that limbers both body and mind. If you are staying near a park or square, look for a group of Taiwanese doing *tai chi* exercises. Just stand toward the back of the group and follow their motions.

Standard athletic wear, including shorts, is acceptable attire for men and women.

**Transportation and Communications**   Taxis are the best means of transportation for visitors to Taipei and other Taiwan cities. In Taipei, because of traffic congestion, leave plenty of time to get where you are going even if it is only a short distance. A good rule of thumb is twice the time you anticipate a similar trip would take in a major U.S. city.

Since most taxi drivers do not speak English, Americans should carry with them the addresses of their destinations written in Chinese. Their hotel concierge or doorman can assist them in this.

Telecommunications are excellent in Taiwan. International direct dialing is available throughout the country and Fax machines are in wide use. International courier services are also widely available.

**Special Considerations**   Although Taiwan is Westernized in many ways, it remains traditionally Chinese. Age is venerated. Social and organizational hierarchy is carefully observed. And men dominate the senior levels of business and government (although there are many professional women, and sometimes family businesses headed by a woman, often a daughter and only child of the patriarch).

The vast majority of Taiwan business enterprises are small in size, and there often are many players competing in a given industry. Accordingly, American exporters may have difficulty in approaching potential Taiwanese customers in an efficient manner. Americans therefore need to give careful attention to their Taiwan marketing strategies.

Taiwan is hugely successful as a producer and exporter of manufactured goods, but its marketing efforts—both at home and abroad—are considered by some observers to be weak. Accordingly, opportunities may exist in Taiwan for Americans who can provide marketing and advertising services.

Pollution control appears to be an especially strong and growing market in Taiwan. Environmental protection, almost totally neglected during years of rapid industrial growth, is now receiving urgent attention.

Colors can be significant. Red is a good luck color and is often worn on holidays and on festive occasions. Gold, signifying money, is another favorite and is often combined with red. Black is often associated with death.

**ENTRY REQUIREMENTS**

Americans on business need a passport, a letter of guarantee from their company, a visa, sufficient funds for the stay, and a ticket and documents for onward travel.

**MONEY**

Taiwan's unit of currency is the New Taiwan dollar, indicated by the symbol NT$. Cash is obtained easily at banks and hotels and, except at night, at currency exchanges at the airport upon arrival. Major credit cards are accepted in hotels and larger shops and restaurants. International travelers checks are accepted at banks, hotels, and some of the larger shops and restaurants.

One U.S. dollar is equal to about NT$25.

**TIPPING**

Tipping is not normally expected in Taiwan unless an extra service has been performed, such as delivery of a message to your room. A tip of NT$10 or more is then appropriate. Porters should be tipped NT$10 per bag. Restaurants and hotels will add a service charge of ten percent to your bills. Taxi drivers normally are not tipped but will appreciate being permitted to keep small change.

**MAJOR HOLIDAYS**

| | |
|---|---|
| New Year's Day, Founding Day | January 1 |
| Half-year closing | January* |
| Chinese New Year | February/March* |
| Youth Day | March 29 |
| Children's and Women's Day | April 4 |
| Tomb-Sweeping Day | April 5 |
| Labor Day | May 1 |
| Dragon-Boat Festival | May* |
| Mid Autumn Festival | August* |
| Confucius's Birthday | September 28 |
| National Day | October 10 |
| Taiwan Restoration Day | October 25 |
| Chiang Kai-shek's Birthday | October 31 |
| Sun Yat-sen's Birthday | November 12 |
| Constitution Day | December 25 |

(Holidays falling on a Sunday are observed on the following day.)

**USEFUL PHRASES**

| English | Chinese Pinyin** | Phonetic Pronunciation |
|---|---|---|
| Hello | Ni hao | Knee how |
| Good morning | Zao shang hao | Tzaow shang how |
| Good evening | Wan shang hao | Wahn shang how |
| Good night | Wan an | Wahn ahn |
| Good-bye | Zai jian | Dzye jee-en |
| Yes | Dui | Doo-ee |
| No | Bu dui | Boo doo-ee |

---

  &#42;  Date varies
&#42;&#42;  Mandarin

| English | Chinese Pinyin | Phonetic Pronunciation |
|---|---|---|
| Please | Qing | Ching |
| How much? | Duo shao? | Doo-oh shah-oh? |
| Thank you | Xie xie | Shee-yeh shee-yeh |
| You're welcome | Bu xie | Boo shee-yeh |
| Cheers | Gan bei | Kahm pie |
| I don't understand | Wo bu dong | Wah boo dong |

## USEFUL TAIWAN CONTACTS

China External Trade Development Council
333 Keelung Road, Section 1
Taipei 10548, Taiwan, Republic of China
TELEPHONE: 886*/2-738-2345
FAX: 886-2-757-6653

Industrial Development and Investment Center
Ministry of Economic Affairs
7 Roosevelt Road, Section 1
Taipei, Taiwan, Republic of China
TELEPHONE: 886-2-394-7213
FAX: 886-2-392-6835

Government Information Office
3 Chung Hsiao East Road, Section 1
Taipei, Taiwan, Republic of China
TELEPHONE: 886-2-341-9211
FAX: 886-2-392-8113

Chinese National Association of Industry and Commerce
390 Fu Hsin South Road, Section 1
Taipei, Taiwan, Republic of China
TELEPHONE: 886-2-707-0111
FAX: 886-2-701-7601

General Chamber of Commerce of the Republic of China
390 Fu Hsin South Road, Section 1
Taipei, Taiwan, Republic of China
TELEPHONE: 886-2-701-2671
FAX: 886-2-754-2107

Coordination Council for North American Affairs
4201 Wisconsin Avenue, N.W.
Washington, DC 20016-2137
TELEPHONE: 202/895-1800
FAX: 202/363-0999

Coordination Council for North American Affairs
2 Midtown Plaza
1349 West Peachtree Street, N.E.
Atlanta, GA 30309
TELEPHONE: 404/872-0123
FAX: 404/873-3474

---

\* Taiwan's country code

Coordination Council for North American Affairs
99 Summer Street
Boston, MA 02110
TELEPHONE: 617/737-2050
FAX: 617/737-2060

Coordination Council for North American Affairs
180 North Stetson Avenue
Chicago, IL 60601
TELEPHONE: 312/616-0100
FAX: 312/616-1490

Coordination Council for North American Affairs
2746 Pali Highway
Honolulu, HI 96817
TELEPHONE: 808/595-6347
FAX: 808/595-6542

Coordination Council for North American Affairs
11 Green Way Plaza
Houston, TX 77046
TELEPHONE: 713/626-7445
FAX: 713/626-1202

Coordination Council for North American Affairs
3100 Broadway
Kansas City, MO 64111
TELEPHONE: 816/531-1298
FAX: 816/531-3066

Coordination Council for North American Affairs
3731 Wilshire Boulevard
Los Angeles, CA 90010
TELEPHONE: 213/389-1215
FAX: 213/383-3245

Coordination Council for North American Affairs
2333 Ponce de Leon Boulevard
Coral Gables, FL 33134
TELEPHONE: 305/443-8917
FAX: 305/444-4796

Coordination Council for North American Affairs
801 Second Avenue
New York, NY 10017
TELEPHONE: 212/370-6600
FAX: 212/370-1674

Coordination Council for North American Affairs
555 Montgomery Street
San Francisco, CA 94111
TELEPHONE: 415/362-7680
FAX: 415/362-5382

Coordination Council for North American Affairs
Westin Building
2001 Sixth Avenue
Seattle, WA 98121
TELEPHONE: 206/441-4586
FAX: 206/441-4320

American Institute in Taiwan
Commercial Section
33 Keelung Road, Section 1
Taipei 10548, Taiwan, Republic of China
TELEPHONE: 886-2-720-1550
FAX: 886-2-757-7162

American Institute in Taiwan
1700 North Moore Street
Arlington, VA 22205
TELEPHONE: 703/625-6474
FAX: 703/841-1385

American Chamber of Commerce in Taipei
96, Chung Shan North Road, Section 2
Taipei 104, Taiwan, Republic of China
TELEPHONE: 886-2-581-7089
FAX: 886-2-542-3376

# COUNTRY PROFILE: THAILAND

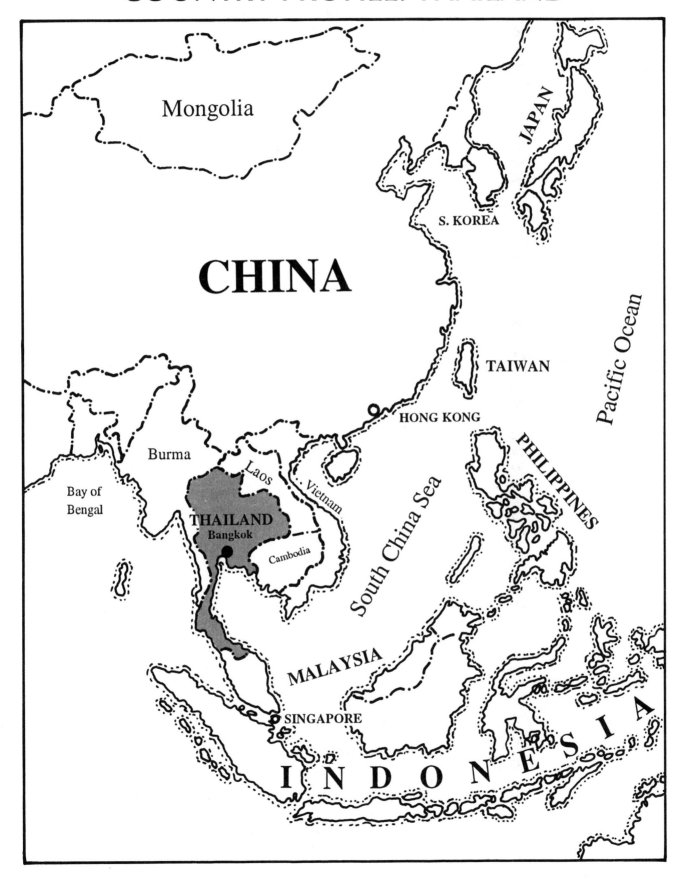

## A THAI ALLIANCE

"For an American company to enter the service business in Asia, we think it's essential for it to have a strategic alliance with an Asian firm," says Pat Loui, President of OmniTrak Group, Inc., of Honolulu, Hawaii. "Not only do you need in-country contacts, you need someone to backstop you when the pressure's on," she adds. "In the service business, timely performance is critical."

OmniTrak is a full service marketing research company with headquarters in Honolulu, offices in Guam and California, and 100 full-time employees.

"By the late 1980s, we saw good opportunities for us in Southeast Asia," says Loui. "The region was growing fast, yet the service industries that we work with—communications, advertising, and public relations—were still in their early stages of development there."

In 1989, OmniTrak formed a joint venture for a full service marketing research firm in Bangkok, Thailand, with Acorn Marketing Research Consultants of Singapore and Dr. Rawewan Prakobpol, a Thai mass communications professor and researcher who was seconded to the Prime Minister's office.

"I knew Rawewan from the time we were both graduate students at the East-West Center in Honolulu, and I had gotten to know Acorn through various marketing research organizations," says Loui. "All three of us saw Thailand as a good opportunity. Its economy was booming, the government had a very pro-business attitude, and there was room for another marketing research firm. For OmniTrak and Acorn, it also met our respective strategic goals of expanding internationally."

"Each of us made an important contribution to the venture," Loui adds. "OmniTrak brought its multi-country experience and United States relationships, Acorn brought Southeast Asian experience and relationships and backstopping capabilities, and Rawewan brought the key ingredient, the Thai connections."

The venture, called Acorn-OmniTrak Marketing and Research Consultants Inc., is now the second largest marketing research firm in Thailand. The company does both consumer and business studies for the private sector. It bases its studies on national samples and on personal interviews and "central location intercepts" (interviews at shopping centers, for example) in metropolitan Bangkok. Principal clients include such multinational corporations as RJR Nabisco, Tupperware, General Motors, Citibank, Procter & Gamble, and Colgate Palmolive. Acorn-Omnitrak has 35 employees.

Loui believes that staff training is critically important for an international service business based in Asia. "We conduct annual region-wide employee development seminars for our professional staff, focusing on field methodology and quality control in data collection for both attitudinal and behavioral research," she says.

There are two essential ingredients in establishing a successful service industry joint venture in Asia, according to Loui. "The first is a partner you can trust. You'll be too far away and too busy to audit the financial details every month," she says. "The second is an excellent local network that includes the governmental and academic communities as well as the business community. In Asia there is a much closer, collaborative relationship among the three than there is in the United States. A good partner will provide access to this three dimensional network."

## THAILAND: ECONOMIC BACKGROUND

In 1991 there was yet another military coup in Thailand, about the sixteenth successful or attempted coup since power was wrested from an absolute monarchy in 1932.

As Yogi Berra would say, "This is déjà vu all over again."

Since 1932, however, despite frequent changes in leadership, Thailand has been governed by a unique collaboration of the Thai military, a strong, centralized bureaucracy, and a revered monarch. The military normally has been content to let the bureaucracy and various politicians run the government. The King, whose real powers are limited, nonetheless exercises considerable influence because he is so loved by the Thai people. His governmental role and indirect powers are even stronger than those of the British throne in England. (Readers may remember that the bloody 1992 pro-democracy riots in Bangkok were quelled following the King's scolding of Prime Minister Suchinda Kraprayoon and his opponent Chamlong Srimuang, as the two kneeled before him.)

The present King of Thailand is Bhumibol Adulyadej, or Rama IX. He is a descendant of Rama IV who was the subject of the book *Anna and the King of Siam*, by Margaret Landon, and the musical comedy and movie *The King and I*. (The name Siam was changed to Thailand, meaning "Land of the Free," in 1939.) Rama IV, who reigned from 1851 to 1868, was a remarkable, farsighted leader who opened the doors of his kingdom to new ideas in science, education, and historical research. Thais deeply resent the portrayal of their beloved Rama IV in *The King and I* as something of a buffoon.

It seems ironic that a country with so many dramatic changes in government leadership would have one of the strongest, fastest growing economies in Asia. Yet Thailand achieved growth rates averaging 12 percent in the period 1988-1990 while maintaining low inflation rates and a stable currency. Exports boomed in the late 1980s. Direct foreign investment, much of it from Japan, jumped 54 percent in 1989. While growth has slowed somewhat, there is every indication that Thailand's strong economic expansion will continue.

The key to Thailand's economic success has been a series of pro-business government administrations that implemented liberal free market development policies. Visitors to Bangkok, bogged down in traffic congestion and confounded by an apparent lack of planning and coordination at every turn, will wonder at Thailand's achievements. However, the chaos they encounter is largely the by-product of Thailand's vitality.

Thailand is a substantial country. It is part of continental Southeast Asia, lying just north of the Malay Peninsula. Thailand is three-fourths the size of Texas but has three times its population (and almost twice the population of California, the United States' most populous state). About 75 percent of the population is ethnic Thai, descended in part from tribes that migrated long ago from southern China. Other ethnic groups include Chinese, Laotians, Vietnamese, Malays, Cambodians, and hill tribe people. Many of these, or their ancestors, entered Thailand as refugees from neighboring countries in times of war.

Thailand is relatively rich in natural resources, with high-yielding agricultural lands and extensive reserves of tin, lead, zinc, potash, and oil and gas. The country is the world's leading exporter of rice and tapioca and a major exporter of rubber, corn, and sugar. There is a large pool of inexpensive labor that enables the country to attract foreign investment for the expansion of export-driven manufacturing industries.

While agriculture employs 65 percent of the working population, manufacturing is now the largest sector of the economy, producing about 25 percent of the gross domestic product compared to agriculture's 17 percent.

Most of Thailand's manufacturing is located in the Bangkok area. Manufacturing expanded there during the 1970s and 1980s from import-substitution activities (producing goods such as beverages and vehicles that otherwise needed to be imported) to export-oriented activities such as the manufacture of clothing, electronics, and chemicals.

Long range government plans are to develop additional manufacturing centers in other parts of Thailand. Two new ports, a petrochemical complex, a fertilizer plant, and export processing zones are planned for the eastern seaboard, southeast of Bangkok. On the services side, the government is pushing the development of tourism (the principal destinations are Chieng-Mai, Pattaya, and Phuket) and promoting Thailand's growing importance as a convention center.

United States commercial interests in Thailand focus on the energy sector, where there are large investments by Unocal, Caltex, and Exxon in refineries and exploration activities. Other U.S. interests are in manufacturing, with extensive production facilities operated by companies such as Seagate Technology, American Telephone and Telegraph, Procter & Gamble, and Pittsburgh Plate Glass.

The most pressing economic challenge for Thailand in the foreseeable future is to build infrastructure quickly enough to keep pace with the rapid expansion of the economy. Severe strains are appearing in the country's port facilities, transportation networks, and electrical generating systems. Existing roads need to be upgraded and new ones built. Expressways are needed to divert congestion from the Bangkok area, and more seaports, airports, and railways are needed.

There are many opportunities for Americans to participate in Thailand's remarkable business boom. Many will be able to market products and services needed for the buildup of Thailand's infrastructure and the expansion of its manufacturing base. As standards of living improve for Thailand's large population, many other American exporters will be able to participate in a rapidly growing Thai consumer market.

## NEAR-TERM OUTLOOK

Political uncertainty, resulting from the 1992 pro-democracy riots in Bangkok, may well cloud the economic environment during 1993 as democratic and pro-military factions in the government continue to vie for power.

Thailand's growth rate, which averaged ten percent in the late 1980s, is likely to fall to seven percent in 1993. However, the manufacturing sector will remain strong, spurred by substantial foreign investment in recent years. Exports of goods and services will grow by twelve percent in 1993, imports by eleven percent.

Foreign and domestic investment in new facilities will ease somewhat in 1993, but the government will continue to fund such pressing infrastructure projects as highway improvements.

Despite a slackening of economic activity in 1993, consumer spending will increase by at least seven percent. Inflation will hold below six percent.

**LANGUAGE**

Thai is the national language of Thailand. The written language is a distinctive script. The language is spoken throughout the country with only minor differences, but various grammatical forms of Thai are used depending on the social status of the persons being addressed.

Several Chinese dialects are spoken in Thailand in addition to Thai and some Malay is spoken in the south.

Many people in business and government speak English.

**RELIGION**

Thailand is 95 percent Buddhist. A small percentage of the population is Muslim (largely in the south), and there are some Christians, Hindus, and Sikhs.

**VITAL ECONOMIC STATISTICS (1991 Estimates)**

| | |
|---|---|
| Population: | 57.6 million |
| Gross Domestic Product | US$ 92.9 billion |
| Income Per Capita | US$ 1,613 |
| Annual Growth Rate | 9 percent |
| Total Imports | US$ 39 billion |
| Total Exports | US$ 27.5 billion |
| U.S. Share of Manufactured Imports | 10.8 percent |
| U.S. Share of Total Exports | 20.4 percent |

**Top Five Imports From U.S.**

Electrical machinery and parts
Non-electrical machinery and parts for industrial use
Chemicals
Aircraft, ships, and components
Textile fibers

**Top Five Exports To U.S.**

Automatic data processing machines and parts
Garments
Integrated circuits
Precious stones, pearls, jewelry
Canned seafood

**Top Three Foreign Investors**

Japan
Taiwan
Hong Kong

**Top Three Trading Partners**

U.S.
Japan
Europe

## BEST EXPORT OPPORTUNITIES FOR AMERICAN FIRMS*

| | |
|---|---|
| **Computer Software and Services** | Applications for banking/finance, manufacturing, trade/distribution, advertising/publishing |
| **Franchising Services** | Auto lube, diagnostic, specialty stores, commercial building cleaning services |
| **Computers and Peripherals** | Mini-computers, workstations, hard disk drives, power regulators such as surge suppressors and uninterruptable power systems |
| **Aircraft and Aircraft Parts** | Long range and mid range aircraft and parts |
| **Electronic Components** | Parts of electronic ICs and micro assemblies, other monolithic ICs |
| **Plastic Materials and Resins** | Polypropylene in primary forms, styrene, polystyrene, other polyethers in primary form, monofilament, rods, sticks and profile shapes of other plastics, artificial guts (sausage casings) of hardened protein |
| **Electric Power Systems** | Steam generating plant equipment, turbine generator plant equipment, burner retrofit |
| **Medical Equipment** | Diagnostic equipment |
| **Electronics Industry Production and Test Equipment** | Electronics equipment for manufacture of electrical appliances, computers and components, telecommunications equipment, electronic ball bearings, integrated circuits |
| **Telecommunications Equipment** | Telephone switching equipment, optical fiber cable, mobile telephone equipment, paging systems, cellular 900 MHz mobile telephones, satellite receiver antennas, radio and TV broadcasting equipment |
| **Chemical Production Equipment** | Solids/liquids/gases handling and transport equipment, pollution control and effluent treatment, water treatment, separation equipment, refinery equipment, pipelines, valves and pumps, process design, simulation and engineering services |
| **Power Transmission Systems** | Substation transmission systems, transmission line conductors, portable switch stations, power transformers, electric drive pumps, automatic switching equipment, fuse cutouts, automatic feeder-voltage regulators |
| **Oil and Gas Field Machinery** | Drilling and boring equipment, geophysical instruments, oil well drill pipes, casing, and tubes |

---

* U.S. Chamber of Commerce 1992 Rankings

| | |
|---|---|
| **Advertising Services** | Institutional advertising, sophisticated ad campaigns, overseas advertising |
| **Architectural/Construction/ Engineering Services** | Electric power generation and transmission, natural gas and petrochemical, golf courses, design/construction of manufacturing plants for private firms from U.S., Japan, Europe |
| **Food Processing and Packaging Equipment** | Food processing and packaging machinery for fruits and vegetables, meat, poultry and eggs, fish and seafood, and fats and pills extraction and processing machinery |
| **Avionics and Ground Support Equipment** | Instrument landing systems, Doppler very high frequency omni-range, distance measure equipment, non-directional beacons, weather radar, flight simulators |
| **Marine Fisheries Products (Seafood)** | Albacore or long finned tuna, skip jack or stripe-bellied bonito, yellow-fin tuna, Pacific salmon |
| **Pumps, Valves, and Compressors** | Fuel pumps for filling stations, centrifugal pumps, gas compressors, parts |
| **Pollution Control Equipment** | Municipal waste water treatment systems, municipal solid waste disposal systems, domestic air cleaning devices, catalytic equipment for automotive exhaust systems |
| **Cosmetics** | Hair care and skin care products |
| **Jewelry** | Jewelry and parts of gold or gold alloy |
| **Construction Equipment** | Machinery for a 360-degree revolving superstructure |
| **Building Products** | Light weight panel and flooring for low cost housing projects, structural systems and materials, finishing products and materials for external façades, interior design and renovation products, M & E and building control systems, admixtures, sealants and compounds, insulation materials, roofing materials, automated production/processing lines for locally made building products, equipment and machinery for civil and infrastructural building projects |
| **Air-Conditioning and Refrigeration Equipment** | Air conditioners above 24,000 BTU |
| **Machine Tools and Metalworking Equipment** | Machining centers, single station construction machine, multi station transfer machine, NC milling machines (knee type), NC flat surface grinding machine, hydraulic press of NLT 1,000 tons capacity |
| **Plastics Production Machinery** | Injection molding equipment, extruders, blow molding, vacuum molding |

| | |
|---|---|
| **Iron and Steel** | Flat-rolled products of iron or non-alloy steel coated with tin, other flat-rolled products, ferrous waste and scrap |
| **Automotive Parts and Service Equipment** | OEM, aftermarket parts for Japanese brand cars, automotive diagnostic, maintenance, repair equipment, auto maintenance and service franchises |
| **Textile Machinery and Equipment** | Carding machines, spinning machines, winding machines for preparing yarns, weaving machines (shuttle and shuttle-less types), knitting, lace, and other specialty machines |
| **Coal** | |

## BUSINESS PRACTICES

### Meetings

Americans should arrange meetings in advance, before arriving in Thailand. Although some Thai organizations are willing to set up meetings with strangers, it is preferable to arrange first-time meetings through an intermediary who knows both parties. This can be done through a colleague, a Thai government office or business association, or a consultant.

While meetings are serious affairs in Thailand, conducting business takes a back seat to social courtesies. Plan to devote a considerable amount of time to genial conversation at the outset of a meeting, especially if it is the first opportunity the parties have had to get acquainted.

Meetings generally are informal. They are commonly held wherever the surroundings are pleasant and convenient, whether in offices, restaurants, clubs, or hotels. First meetings are often entirely social and held over luncheon, cocktails, or dinner. Business breakfasts are not common.

It is important for Americans to observe punctuality, but they should not be surprised if Thais are late to meetings. In setting meeting times in Bangkok, Americans should be sensitive to commuting problems caused by (serious) traffic congestion. They should not request meetings that commence in the early morning or end in the late afternoon.

Plan for meetings to last much longer than they would in the United States.

### Business Hours

Offices normally are open five days a week, Monday through Friday, from 8:30 a.m. to 5 p.m. Luncheon is taken at noon.

### Greetings

The normal greeting in Thailand is the *wai*, given with palms together and fingers up at the chest or higher and with a slight bow. Thai business people, especially men, also shake hands. When greeting a Thai, an American should pause to see which greeting the Thai chooses and then follow suit.

The *wai* is given with the hands raised higher and the bow made lower than normal when greeting persons of higher social standing or greater age.

The *wai* is used on departing as well as in greeting.

### Business Cards

Business cards should always be exchanged in Thailand on first meeting. It is not expected that an American's cards will be printed in Thai on one side, but such a gesture is considered thoughtful and is appreciated.

**Names and Titles**  Few Thais used family names until the 1920s when King Rama VI decreed that they should. All Thais now have family names (placed last in sequence, Western style), but they invariably go by their given names and consider it odd if addressed by the family name. Americans therefore should address Thais by their first names in all circumstances.

Khun (pronounced koon) is used in place of "Mr.," "Mrs.," "Miss," or "Dr." (as in Khun Amnuay). Americans should not be surprised to be addressed by their first names in Thailand (as in Khun Robert or Khun Mary). Indeed, they should expect to be addressed this way.

Titles are seldom used in addressing business people in Thailand. Thais are not addressed, for example, as "Vice President Kaset" or "Engineer Prasong."

**Clothing**  Lightweight business suits with ties and white or off-color shirts are the normal attire for business men in Thailand. Safari-style suits also are worn. Suits or dresses are the norm for business women. Jackets are doffed in meetings when temperatures are warm. Jackets are required at some restaurants. Neither jackets nor ties are otherwise required for informal wear.

**Gifts and Entertainment**  Gift-giving is not as widely practiced in Thailand as in many other Asian nations. Thoughtful (but not lavish) gifts are appropriate when an important business relationship is developing. Good gifts in these circumstances are pens or other useful items bearing your organization's logo. Something associated with your part of the United States also makes a good gift. Gifts should be presented graciously and not casually, and do not insist that your gift be opened in your presence.

Thais normally entertain in restaurants. When Americans are entertained at a Thai home, it is appropriate to give the host and hostess a basket of fruit or a tin of cakes or cookies. Americans can easily entertain their Thai friends at hotels. If a dinner is arranged, it is appropriate to invite the spouses of the Thai guests.

**Conversation**  Family and personal matters are favorite topics for Thais. Americans will be asked questions that might be considered offensive in the United States, such as what is their age and how much do they earn. This is characteristic of the Thai collectivist culture and hierarchical society. Thais need to relate to others on a personal level and to understand where others stand in a stratified social structure.

Other good topics for Americans are found in expressing their positive impressions of Thailand and obtaining recommendations for sightseeing, shopping, and restaurants. Discussion of political issues, religion, and the Royal Family should be avoided, and critical remarks should not be made on any subject. *The King and I* should not be mentioned favorably because Thais believe it tends to ridicule their revered King Rama IV.

**Hotels**  Thailand's cities have many excellent hotels with great facilities and service. Reservations should be made well in advance, especially if visiting during the tourist high season (September to March).

In Bangkok, because of traffic congestion, try to choose a hotel that is convenient to your business appointments.

**Exercise**  The larger Bangkok hotels have excellent swimming pools and exercise facilities for their guests. There also are health clubs in the city with good facilities.

Jogging and walking are good forms of exercise *if* traffic congestion and automobile exhaust can be avoided. In Bangkok, there are a number of fine parks and wooded paths, some on hotel grounds, that are popular jogging sites for Thais and visitors alike.

Standard athletic wear, including shorts, is acceptable attire for men and women.

**Transportation and Communications**  Taxis are plentiful and inexpensive in Thailand. They are by far the best means of transportation for visitors to Bangkok and other Thai cities.

Taxi drivers seldom speak English, so you should carry with you, written in Thai, the addresses of your destinations. Also, since taxis seldom have meters, it is necessary to bargain for the fare before the ride begins. The fare can be indicated with your fingers (two fingers is B20, five is B50, etc.). Your hotel concierge or doorman can assist you in writing down addresses and arranging fares.

In Bangkok, because of traffic congestion, you must allow plenty of time to get where you are going even if it is only a short distance. This "warning" really cannot be overstated.

Telecommunications are good in hotels and offices in Thailand but are only inconsistently available elsewhere. Fax machines and international courier services are available.

**Special Considerations**  There are trading impediments associated with doing business in Thailand. Tariffs are still high on some goods. (The trade-weighted average is 23 percent.) Intellectual property rights protection is inadequate, although laws and law enforcement are improving. Import and licensing procedures are inefficient. There is also is a considerable amount of lower level graft and fraud.

When dealing with Thais, Americans should give close attention to being thoughtful and considerate and to demonstrating a generous nature. These are qualities that are especially important in Thailand. Americans should not be excessive in this regard, however. For Thais, it is the thoughtfulness and appropriateness of a gesture that is important.

Thailand is known as the "Land of Smiles." Americans will find that smiling, even in the face of adversity, will accomplish much more than logic or insistence. The popular Thai expression *mai pen rai* ("never mind; it doesn't matter") is one that expresses harmony, not resignation.

Conversely, Americans will find that losing their temper and displaying anger will have a negative, unproductive impact in Thailand.

Although Thailand's constitution gives women fully equal rights with men, Thai women are traditionally submissive toward men. Accordingly, there are few women in the senior ranks of business and government. However, there are many women in the professions and many who are active in efforts to improve women's rights.

While Bangkok is generally safe for visitors, some theft, pick pocketing, and burglary goes on in parts of the city and on public conveyances.

Visitors should take the usual precautions to guard their personal belongings: lock the windows of your room when going out, place special valuables in a hotel safe (and get an itemized receipt), and wear a money belt if walking in crowded areas.

Thais are especially sensitive to body language and colors. One should avoid touching a Thai, especially on the head. A woman should not touch or hand something directly to a Buddhist monk. Pointing fingers or toes toward a Thai is offensive. Colors have various meanings, some positive, some negative.

Prostitution is a thriving industry in Thailand, and AIDS is a serious health problem in the country, especially in the north.

## ENTRY REQUIREMENTS

Americans on business need a passport, a visa, sufficient funds for the stay, and a ticket and documents for onward travel.

## MONEY

Thailand's unit of currency is the *baht*, indicated by the symbol B. Major credit cards are accepted in hotels and larger shops and restaurants. International travelers checks are accepted at banks and hotels. Cash may be obtained at currency exchanges at the airport upon arrival (except at night) and at banks and hotels. However, exchange rates for money and travelers checks at hotels tend to be unfavorable.

One U.S. dollar is equal to about B25.

## TIPPING

Tipping has not been a common practice among Thais, but it is now expected of overseas visitors. Americans should plan to tip for personal services. Tips up to B50 are appropriate for bellhops and room service waiters, and others who perform small services. Porters should be tipped about B5 per bag. Restaurants and hotels normally will add a ten percent service charge to your bills. Taxi drivers normally need not be tipped, but a hotel driver should be tipped about B50. Small change may be tipped in some situations, but not merely B1, which would be considered an insult.

## MAJOR HOLIDAYS

| | |
|---|---|
| New Year's Day | January 1 |
| Makha Bucha Day | February* |
| Chakri Memorial Day | April 6 |
| Songkran Festival Day | April* |
| Labor Day | May 1 |
| Coronation Day | May 5 |
| Visakha Bucha Day | May/June* |
| Queen's Birthday | August 12 |
| Chulalongkorn Day | October 23 |
| King's Birthday | December 5 |
| Constitution Day | December 10 |
| New Year's Eve | December 31 |

(Holidays falling on a Saturday or Sunday are normally observed on the following Monday.)

---

* Date varies

| USEFUL PHRASES | English | Thai | Phonetic Pronunciation |
|---|---|---|---|
| | Hello | Sawat dee khrap (to a man) | Sah-waht dee kahp |
| | | Sawat dee kha (to a woman) | Sah-waht dee khah |
| | Good morning | (same) | (same) |
| | Good evening | (same) | (same) |
| | Good night | (same) | (same) |
| | Good-bye | (same) | (same) |
| | Yes | Khrap (to a man) | Kahp |
| | | Kha (to a woman) | Kah |
| | No | Mai khrap (to a man) | My kahp |
| | | Mai kha (to a woman) | My kah |
| | Please | Dai prod | Dye prod |
| | How much? | Taorai? | Ta-oh-rye? |
| | Thank you | Khob khun khrap (to a man) | Cob koon kahp |
| | | Khob khun kha (to a woman) | Cob koon kahp |
| | You're welcome | Yindee | Yin-dee |
| | Cheers | Chaiyo | Shay-yoh |
| | I don't understand | Pom mai kaojai (to a man) | Pom my-kah-o-jye |
| | | Dichan maikaojai (to a woman) | Dee-chahn my-kah-o-jye |
| | Never mind | Mai pen rai | My pen rye |

**USEFUL THAILAND CONTACTS**

Ministry of Commerce
Foreign Trade Department
Sanamchai Road
Bangkok 10200, Thailand
TELEPHONE: 66*/2-223-1481
FAX: 66-2-226-3318

Board of Trade of Thailand
Ministry of Interior
150 Rajbopit Road
Bangkok 10200, Thailand
TELEPHONE: 66-2-221-1827
FAX: 66-2-225-3995

Ministry of Finance
Customs Department
Sunthornkosa Road
Bangkok, Thailand
TELEPHONE: 66-2-249-0431
FAX: 66-2-249-2874

Ministry of Industry
Industrial Promotion Department
Rama VI Road
Bangkok, Thailand
TELEPHONE: 66-2-246-1031
FAX: 66-2-247-8004

---

\*   Thailand's country code

Thai Chamber of Commerce
150 Rajbopit Road
Bangkok 10200, Thailand
TELEPHONE: 66-2-225-0086
FAX: 66-2-225-3372

U.S. Embassy
Commercial Section
Diethelm Tower A
93/1 Wireless Road
Bangkok 10330, Thailand
TELEPHONE: 66-2-255-4365
FAX: 66-2-255-2915

American Chamber of Commerce in Thailand
Kian Gwan Building
140 Wireless Road
Bangkok, Thailand
TELEPHONE: 66-2-251-9266
FAX: 66-2-255-2454

# APPENDICES

# APPENDIX A: RESOURCE ORGANIZATIONS

Set forth below are the principal government offices that provide information and services to Americans interested in exporting to Asia.

## U.S. Department of Commerce

The Commerce Department administers a vast array of programs and assistance designed to promote U.S. exports.

**TRADE INFORMATION CENTER,** a one-stop source of information on all federal government export assistance programs.

TELEPHONE: 800/USA-TRADE (800/872-8723)

**TRADE OPPORTUNITIES PROGRAM** provides current sales leads.

TELEPHONE: 202/377-1986
FAX: 202/377-2164

**INDUSTRY SPECIALISTS** provide information relating to specific industries.

TELEPHONE: 202/377-1461
FAX: 202/377-5697

**COUNTRY DESK OFFICERS** provide current information on specific countries.

TELEPHONE: 202/482-3875

**JAPAN EXPORT INFORMATION CENTER** provides assistance relating to exports to Japan.

TELEPHONE: 202/377-2425
FAX: 202/377-0469

**JAPAN UNITED OVERSEAS DEVELOPMENT ASSISTANCE PROGRAM** tracks procurement opportunities involving Japan's foreign aid programs.

TELEPHONE: 202/377-4002
FAX: 202/377-0316

**MULTILATERAL DEVELOPMENT BANK** tracks procurement opportunities involving the Asia Development Bank.

TELEPHONE: 202/377-4333
FAX: 202/377-3954

**OFFICE OF EXPORT LICENSING** provides licensing assistance.

TELEPHONE: 202/377-8536; 202/377-4811
FAX: 202/377-3322

**OFFICE OF INTERNATIONAL MAJOR PROJECTS** tracks opportunities involving overseas infrastructure and industrial projects.

TELEPHONE: 202/377-5225
FAX: 202/377-3954

**OFFICE OF MULTILATERAL AFFAIRS** provides information on trade policies.

TELEPHONE: 202/377-0603
FAX: 202/377-5939

**FISHERIES PROMOTION AND TRADE** provides assistance relating to fisheries.

TELEPHONE: 301/731-2379
FAX: 301/588-4853

**INTERNATIONAL TRADE ADMINISTRATION OFFICES** provides a full range of information and services.

Herbert Clark Hoover Building
14th and Constitution Avenue, N.W.
Washington, DC 20230
TELEPHONE: 202/377-3181
FAX: 202/377-5270

Berry Building
2015 2nd Avenue North
Birmingham, AL 35203
TELEPHONE: 205/731-1331
FAX: 205/731-0076

World Trade Center Alaska
4201 Tudor Center Drive
Anchorage, AK 99508
TELEPHONE: 907/261-4237
FAX: 907/261-4242

Federal Building
230 North 1st Avenue
Phoenix, AZ 85025
TELEPHONE: 602/379-3285
FAX: 602/379-4324

Savers Federal Building
320 West Capitol Avenue
Little Rock, AR 72201
TELEPHONE: 501/378-5794
FAX: 501/324-7380

11000 Wilshire Boulevard
Los Angeles, CA 90024
TELEPHONE: 213/575-7104
FAX: 213/575-7220

6363 Greenwich Drive
San Diego, CA 92122
TELEPHONE: 619/557-5395
FAX: 619557-6176

116-A West 4th Street
Santa Ana, CA 92701
TELEPHONE: 714/836-2461
FAX: 714/836-2330

Federal Building
250 Montgomery Street
San Francisco, CA 94104
TELEPHONE: 415/705-2300
FAX: 415/705-2299

1625 Broadway
Denver, CO 80202
TELEPHONE: 303/844-3246
FAX: 303/844-5651

Federal Building
450 Main Street
Hartford, CT 06103
TELEPHONE: 203/240-3530
FAX: 203/240-3473

128 North Osceola Avenue
Clearwater, FL 34615
TELEPHONE: 813/461-0011
FAX: 813/449-2889

Federal Building
51 S.W. First Avenue
Miami, FL 33130
TELEPHONE: 305/536-5267
FAX: 305/536-4765

Collins Building
107 West Gaines Street
Tallahassee, FL 32304
TELEPHONE: 904/488-6469
FAX: 904/487-1407

Plaza Square North
4360 Chamblee-Dunwoody Road
Atlanta, GA 30341
TELEPHONE: 404/452-9101
FAX: 404/452-9105

120 Barnard Street
Savannah, GA 31401
TELEPHONE: 912/944-4204
FAX: 912/944-4241

400 Ala Moana Boulevard
Honolulu, HI 96850
TELEPHONE: 808/541-1782
FAX: 808/541-3435

Joe R. Williams Building
700 West State Street
Boise, ID 83720
TELEPHONE: 208/334-3857
FAX: 208/334-2631

55 East Monroe Street
Chicago, IL 60603
TELEPHONE: 312/353-4450
FAX: 312/886-8025

515 North Court Street
Rockford, IL 61110-0247
TELEPHONE: 815/987-8123
FAX: 815/987-8122

One North Capitol
Indianapolis, IN 46204
TELEPHONE: 317/226-6214
FAX: 317/226-6139

424 First Avenue N.E.
Cedar Rapids, IA 52401
TELEPHONE: 319/362-8418
FAX: 319/398-5228

Federal Building
210 Walnut Street
Des Moines, IA 50309
TELEPHONE: 515/284-4222
FAX: 515/284-4021

151 N. Volutsia
Wichita, KS 67214-4695
TELEPHONE: 316/269-6160
FAX: 316/262-5652

Gene Snyder Courthouse
601 West Broadway
Louisville, KY 40202
TELEPHONE: 502/582-5066
FAX: 502/582-6573

World Trade Center
#2 Canal Street
New Orleans, LA 70130
TELEPHONE: 504/589-6546
FAX: 504/586-2337

77 Sewall Street
Augusta, ME 04330
TELEPHONE: 207/622-8249
FAX: 207/626-9156

U.S. Customhouse
40 South Gay Street
Baltimore, MD 21202
TELEPHONE: 301/962-3560
FAX: 301/962-7813

World Trade Center
Commonwealth Pier
Boston, MA 02210
TELEPHONE: 617/565-8563
FAX: 617/565-8530

McNamara Building
477 Michigan Avenue
Detroit, MI 48226
TELEPHONE: 313/226-3650
FAX: 313/226-3657

300 Monroe N.W.
Grand Rapids, MI 49503
TELEPHONE: 616/456-2411
FAX: 616/456-2695

Federal Building
110 South 4th Street
Minneapolis, MN 55401
TELEPHONE: 612/348-1638
FAX: 612/348-1650

Jackson Mall Office Center
300 Woodrow Wilson Boulevard
Jackson, MS 39213
TELEPHONE: 601/965-4388
FAX: 601/965-5386

601 East 12th Street
Kansas City, MO 64106
TELEPHONE: 816/426-3141
FAX: 816/426-3140

7911 Forsyth Boulevard
St. Louis, MO 63105
TELEPHONE: 314/425-3302
FAX: 314/425-3381

11133 "O" Street
Omaha, NE 68137
TELEPHONE: 402/221-3664
FAX: 402/221-3668

1755 East Plumb Lane
Reno, NV 89502
TELEPHONE: 702/784-5203
FAX: 702/784-5343

3131 Princeton Pike Building
Trenton, NJ 08648
TELEPHONE: 609/989-2100
FAX: 609/989-2395

625 Silver S.W.
Albuquerque, NM 87102
TELEPHONE: 505/766-2070
FAX: 505/766-1057

Federal Building
111 West Huron Street
Buffalo, NY 14202
TELEPHONE: 716/846-4191
FAX: 716/846-5290

26 Federal Plaza
New York, NY 10278
TELEPHONE: 212/264-0600
FAX: 212/264-1356

111 East Avenue
Rochester, NY 14604
TELEPHONE: 716/263-6480
FAX: 716/325-6505

400 West Market Street
Greensboro, NC 27401
TELEPHONE: 919/333-5345
FAX: 919/333-5158

Federal Building
550 Main Street
Cincinnati, OH 45202
TELEPHONE: 513/684-2944
FAX: 513/684-3200

668 Euclid Avenue
Cleveland, OH 44114
TELEPHONE: 216/522-4750
FAX: 216/522-2235

6601 Broadway Extension
Oklahoma City, OK 73116
TELEPHONE: 405/231-5302
FAX: 405/841-5245

440 South Houston Street
Tulsa, OK 74127
TELEPHONE: 918/581-7650
FAX: 918/581-2844

One World Trade Center
121 S.W. Salmon
Portland, OR 97204
TELEPHONE: 503/326-3001
FAX: 503/326-6351

475 Allendale Road
King of Prussia, PA 19406
TELEPHONE: 717/386-3580
FAX: 717/386-2232

Federal Building
1000 Liberty Avenue
Pittsburgh, PA 15222
TELEPHONE: 412/644-2850
FAX: 412/644-4875

7 Jackson Walkway
Providence, RI 02903
TELEPHONE: 401/528-5104
FAX: 401/528-5067

J. C. Long Building
9 Liberty Street
Charleston, SC 29424
TELEPHONE: 803/727-4361
FAX: 803/792-5697

Strom Thurmond Federal Building
1835 Assembly Street
Columbia, SC 29201
TELEPHONE: 803/765-5345
FAX: 803/253-3614

301 East Church Avenue
Knoxville, TN 37915
TELEPHONE: 615/545-4637
FAX: 615/523-2071

Falls Building
22 North Front Street
Memphis, TN 38103
TELEPHONE: 901/544-4137
FAX: 901/675-3510

Parkway Towers
404 James Robertson Parkway
Nashville, TN 37219-1505
TELEPHONE: 615/736-5161
FAX: 615/736-2454

816 Congress Street
Austin, TX 78711
TELEPHONE: 512/482-5939
FAX: 512/320-9674

World Trade Center
2060 North Stemmore Freeway, S. 170
Dallas, TX 75242-0787
TELEPHONE: 214/767-0542
FAX: 214/767-8240

515 Rusk Street
Houston, TX 77002
TELEPHONE: 713/229-2578
FAX: 713/229-2203

324 South State Street
Salt Lake City, UT 84111
TELEPHONE: 801/524-5116
FAX: 801/524-5886

Federal Building
400 North 8th Street
Richmond, VA 23240
TELEPHONE: 804/771-2246
FAX: 804/771-2390

3131 Elliott Avenue
Seattle, WA 98121
TELEPHONE: 206/553-5615
FAX: 206/553-7253

405 Capitol Street
Charleston, WV 25301
TELEPHONE: 304/347-5123
FAX: 304/347-5408

517 East Wisconsin Avenue
Milwaukee, WI 53202
TELEPHONE: 414/297-3473
FAX: 414/297-3470

## U.S. Small Business Administration

The SBA provides information, training, and export financing for smaller U.S. businesses.

**OFFICE OF INTERNATIONAL TRADE**
409 Third Street, S.W.
Washington, DC 20416
TELEPHONE: 202/205-6720
FAX: 202/205-7272

**SBA REGIONAL OFFICES**

71 Stevenson Street
San Francisco, CA 94105-2939
TELEPHONE: 415/744-6402
FAX: 415/744-6435

999 18th Street
Denver, CO 80202
TELEPHONE: 303/294-7186
FAX: 303/294-7153

1375 Peachtree Street, N.E.
Atlanta, GA 30367-8102
TELEPHONE: 404/347-2797
FAX: 404/347-2355

300 South Riverside Plaza
Chicago, IL 60606-6617
TELEPHONE: 312/353-5000
FAX: 312/353-3426

155 Federal Street
Boston, MA 02110
TELEPHONE: 617/451-2023
FAX: 617/565-8695

911 Walnut Street
Kansas City, MO 64106
TELEPHONE: 816/426-3608
FAX: 816/426-5559

26 Federal Plaza
New York, NY 10278
TELEPHONE: 212/264-1450
FAX: 212/264-0900

475 Allendale Road
King of Prussia, PA 19406
TELEPHONE: 215/962-3700
FAX: 215/962-3743

8625 King George Drive
Dallas, TX 75235-3391
TELEPHONE: 214/767-7633
FAX: 214/767-7870

2615 4th Avenue
Seattle, WA 98121
TELEPHONE: 206/553-5676
FAX: 206/553-4155

## U.S. Department of Agriculture

AGEXPORT CONNECTIONS provides information on opportunities for export of food and agricultural products.

TELEPHONE: 202/720-7103
FAX: 202/690-4374

TRADE ASSISTANCE PLANNING OFFICE provides overseas market information and exporting assistance to agricultural exporters.

TELEPHONE: 703/305-2771
FAX: 703/305-2788

## U.S. Department of Energy

EXPORT ASSISTANCE INITIATIVE identifies energy-related export opportunities.

TELEPHONE: 202/586-0153
FAX: 202/586-3047

## U.S. Department of State

COUNTRY DESK OFFICERS provide country-specific economic and political analyses.

TELEPHONE: 202/647-6575

## U.S. Agency for International Development

CENTER FOR TRADE AND INVESTMENT SERVICES provides information about trade and investment opportunities in the development world.

TELEPHONE: 202/647-3805
FAX: 202/647-1805

## U.S. Export-Import Bank

SERVICES FOR SMALL BUSINESS offers information on export credit insurance, and provides loans to finance sales of U.S. goods and services abroad.

TELEPHONE: 800/424-5201; 213/575-7425
FAX: 213/575-7428

## U.S. Overseas Private Investment Corporation

INVESTOR INFORMATION SERVICE provides economic and political data and information on investment opportunities.

TELEPHONE: 202/457-7128
FAX: 202/833-3375

INVESTOR SERVICES is organized to assist U.S. firms with overseas investment planning and implementation.

TELEPHONE: 202/457-7091
FAX: 202/833-3375

## U.S. Trade Representative

The USTR provides information on trade barriers and unfair trade practices.

TELEPHONE: 202/395-3230
FAX: 202/395-3911

## State Government Trade Offices

Alabama Development Office
401 Adams Avenue
Montgomery, AL 36130
TELEPHONE: 205/242-0400
FAX: 205/242-0486

Office of International Trade
State of Alaska, DECD
3601 C Street
Anchorage, AK 99503
TELEPHONE: 907/561-5585
FAX: 907/561-4577

Office of Business and Trade
Arizona Department of Commerce
3800 N. Central
Phoenix, AZ 85012
TELEPHONE: 602/280-1300
FAX: 602/280-1305

Arkansas Industrial Development Commission
One State Capitol Mall
Little Rock, AR 72201
TELEPHONE: 501/682-7678
FAX: 501/682-7691

California State World Trade Commission
1121 L Street
Sacramento, CA 95814
TELEPHONE: 916/324-5511
FAX: 916/324-5791

International Trade Office
Governor's Office of Economic Development
1625 Broadway
Denver, CO 80202
TELEPHONE: 303/892-3850
FAX: 303/892-3820

International Division
Connecticut Department of Economic Development
865 Brook Street
Rocky Hill, CT 06067
TELEPHONE: 203/258-4256
FAX: 203/529-0535

Delaware Office of Business Development and International Trade
820 French Street
Wilmington, DE 19899
TELEPHONE: 302/577-6262
FAX: 302/577-3027

Bureau of International Trade Development
Florida Department of Commerce
107 West Gaines Street
Tallahassee, FL 32301
TELEPHONE: 904/488-9050
FAX: 904/487-1407

Trade Division
Georgia Department of Industry, Trade, and Tourism
285 Peachtree Center Avenue, NE
P.O. Box 1776
Atlanta, GA 30301-1776
TELEPHONE: 404/656-0633
FAX: 404/651-6505

Products and Services Branch
Hawaii Dept. of Business, Economic Development and Tourism
P.O. Box 2359
Honolulu, HI 96804
TELEPHONE: 808/587-2717
FAX: 808/587-2777

Division of International Business
Idaho State Department of Commerce
700 West State Street
Boise, ID 83720
TELEPHONE: 208/334-2470
FAX: 208/334-2631

International Business Division
Illinois Department of Commerce and Community Affairs
100 West Randolph
Chicago, IL 60601
TELEPHONE: 312/814-7166
FAX: 312/814-6581

International Trade Division
Indiana Department of Commerce
One North Capitol
Indianapolis, IN 46204-2248
TELEPHONE: 317/232-8845
FAX: 317/232-4146

International Division
Iowa Department of Economic Development
200 East Grand Avenue
Des Moines, IA 50309
TELEPHONE: 515/242-4743
FAX: 515/242-4918

Trade Development Division
Kansas Department of Commerce
400 West 8th Street
Topeka, KS 66603
TELEPHONE: 913/296-4027
FAX: 913/296-5263

Office of International Marketing
Kentucky Cabinet for Economic Development
Capitol Plaza Tower
Frankfort, KY 40601
TELEPHONE: 502/564-2170
FAX: 502/564-7697

Louisiana Office of International Trade, Finance and Development
P.O. Box 94185
Baton Rouge, LA 70804-9185
TELEPHONE: 504/342-4320
FAX: 504/342-5389

Maine World Trade Association
77 Sewall Street
Augusta, ME 04330
TELEPHONE: 207/622-0234
FAX: 207/622-3760

Maryland International Division
World Trade Center
401 East Pratt Street
Baltimore, MD 21202
TELEPHONE: 301/333-8180
FAX: 301/333-4302

Massachusetts Office of International Trade
100 Cambridge Street
Boston, MA 02202
TELEPHONE: 617/367-1830
FAX: 617/227-3488

Michigan International Office
P.O. Box 30025
Lansing, MI 48909
TELEPHONE: 517/373-6390
FAX: 517/335-2521

Minnesota Trade Office
Minnesota World Trade Center
30 East 7th Street
St. Paul, MN 55101-4902
TELEPHONE: 612/297-4222
FAX: 612296-3555

Mississippi Department of Economic Development
Walter Sillers Building
550 High Street
Jackson, MS 39201-1113
TELEPHONE: 601/359-6672
FAX: 601/359-2832

International Business Office
State of Missouri
301 West High Street
Jefferson City, MO 65102
TELEPHONE: 314/751-4999
FAX: 314/751-7384

International Trade Office
Montana Department of Commerce
1424 9th Avenue
Helena, MT 59620
TELEPHONE: 406/444-3923
FAX: 406/444-2808

International Development
Nebraska Department of Economic Development
P.O. Box 94666, State Capitol
Lincoln, NE 68509
TELEPHONE: 402/471-3770
FAX: 402/471-3778

Nevada Commission on Economic Development
Capitol Complex
Carson City, NV 89710
TELEPHONE: 702/687-4325
FAX: 702/687-4450

New Hampshire Dept. of Resources and Economic
    Development
105 Loudon Road
Concord, NH 03301
TELEPHONE: 603/271-2591
FAX: 603/271-2629

New Jersey Office of International Trade
153 Halsey Street
Newark, NJ 07101
TELEPHONE: 201/648-3518
FAX: 201/623-1287

Office of International Development
New Mexico Economic Development and Tourism
    Department
Montoya Building
1100 St. Francis Drive
Santa Fe, NM 87503
TELEPHONE: 505/827-0309
FAX: 505/827-0263

International Division
New York State Department of Commerce
1515 Broadway
New York, NY 10036
TELEPHONE: 212/827-6200
FAX: 212/827-6263

International Division
North Carolina Department of Commerce
430 North Salisbury Street
Raleigh, NC 27611
TELEPHONE: 919/733-7193
FAX: 919/733-0110

North Dakota International Trade Division
Liberty Memorial Building
604 East Boulevard Avenue
Bismarck, ND 58505-0820
TELEPHONE: 701/221-5333
FAX: 701/221-5320

International Trade Division
Ohio Department of Development
77 South High Street
Columbus, OH 43215
TELEPHONE: 614/466-5017
FAX: 614/463-1540

International Division
Oklahoma Department of Commerce
6601 Broadway Extension
Oklahoma City, OK 73126-8214
TELEPHONE: 405/843-9770
FAX: 405/841-5245

International Trade Division
Oregon Economic Development Department
One World Trade Center
121 S.W. Salmon
Portland, OR 97204
TELEPHONE: 503/229-5625; 800/452-7813
FAX: 503/222-5050

Office of International Development
Pennsylvania Department of Commerce
Forum Building
Harrisburg, PA 17120
TELEPHONE: 717/787-7190
FAX: 717/234-4560

Rhode Island Department of Economic Development
7 Jackson Walkway
Providence, RI 02903
TELEPHONE: 401/277-2601
FAX: 401/277-2102

South Carolina State Development Board
P.O. Box 927
Columbia, SC 29202
TELEPHONE: 803/737-0400
FAX: 803/737-0418

South Dakota Economic Development and Tourism
711 East Wells Avenue
Pierre, SD 57501-3369
TELEPHONE: 605/773-5032
FAX: 605/773-3256

Tennessee Department of Economic and Community
    Development
320 Sixth Avenue, North
Nashville, TN 37219
TELEPHONE: 615/741-5870
FAX: 615/741-5829

Office of International Trade
Texas Department of Commerce
816 Congress
Austin, TX 78711
TELEPHONE: 512/472-5059
FAX: 512/320-9674

International Marketing
Utah Department of Community and Economic Development
324 South State Street
Salt Lake City, UT 84114
TELEPHONE: 801/538-8736
FAX: 801/538-8889

International Business and Industrial Training
Vermont Department of Economic Development
Pavilion Office Building
109 State Street
Montpelier, VT 05602
TELEPHONE: 802/828-3221
FAX: 802/828-3258

Virginia Department of Economic Development
Two James Center
Richmond, VA 23208-0798
TELEPHONE: 804/371-8242
FAX: 804/371-8860

State of Washington Dept. of Trade and Economic
    Development
2001 Sixth Avenue
Seattle, WA 98121
TELEPHONE: 206/464-7143
FAX: 206/464-7222

West Virginia Governor's Office of Economic and
    Community Development
Building 6
Charleston, WV 25305
TELEPHONE: 304/348-2234
FAX: 304/348-0449

Bureau of International Development
Wisconsin Department of Economic and Community
    Development
123 West Washington Avenue
Madison, WI 53703
TELEPHONE: 608/266-1767
FAX: 608/266-5551

Wyoming Department of Commerce
Economic and Community Development Division
Cheyenne, WY 82002
TELEPHONE: 307/777-7284
FAX: 307/777-5840

# APPENDIX B: TRADE SHOWS

The following are a number of recent or planned Asian trade shows of interest to American exporters.

**AGRO EXPO CHINA '92** (agricultural machinery), April 1992, Beijing, China

**AGROTECH/ANIMALTECH/AQUATECH/DAIRY TECH** (agriculture, animal husbandry, aquaculture technology, dairy technology), February 1993, Bangkok, Thailand

**AIR VEX '92** (air-conditioning, ventilation, heating, and refrigeration), May 1992, Hong Kong

**AMERICA WEEK '92** (various products and services), July 1992, Hong Kong

**ASIA HARDWARE/FASTENER** (fastener production and hardware), July 1992, Singapore

**ASIA LEATHER FAIR** (leather machinery), August 1992, Singapore

**ASIA REALBUILD** (construction technology), March 1993, Bangkok, Thailand

**ASIA WELDEX** (welding surface treatments), July 1992, Singapore

**ASIAN AEROSPACE '92** (commercial and military aircraft systems and services), February 1992, Singapore

**ASIAN INTERNATIONAL GIFT FAIR '92** (gifts and handicraft items), May 1992, Singapore

**BREW DRINK TECH ASIA** (brewing and drink manufacturing technology), March 1993, Singapore

**BUILDING SERVICES** (mechanical and electrical services), October 1993, Singapore

**BUSINESS SHOW OSAKA '93** (office and data processing equipment), May 1993, Osaka, Japan

**CATT** (computer aided technologies), August 1992, Bangkok, Thailand

**COSMETICS HAIR AND BEAUTY '92**, June 1992, Hong Kong

**COMPUTECH** (computer technology), February 1993, Surabaya, Indonesia

**DEFENSE SERVICES ASIA** (military equipment and services), April 1992, Kuala Lumpur, Malaysia

**ENTECH ASEAN** (environmental technology), June 1993, Bangkok, Thailand

**EXPOCHEM ASIA** (industrial organic/inorganic and agricultural chemicals), July 1994, Manila, The Philippines

**FOOD AND HOTEL ASIA '92** (equipment and supplies for hotel, restaurant, and catering industries), April 1992, Singapore

**FOODEX JAPAN** (food and beverage), March 1993, Tokyo, Japan

**FOODEX BANGKOK** (food and catering equipment), September 1992, Bangkok, Thailand

**FOODTECH BANGKOK** (food technology), February 1993, Bangkok, Thailand

**FRANCHISE ASIA** (franchising), May 1994, Singapore

**GLOBALTRONICS '92** (electronic components and equipment), September 1992, Singapore

**HOTELEX** (hotel and restaurant equipment), September 1992, Bangkok, Thailand

**HRD ASIA** (human resources development), November 1992, Singapore

**HRD JAPAN** (human resources development), February 1993, Tokyo, Japan

**IMAC** (industrial measurement technology), June 1993, Bangkok, Thailand

**INCHEM** (chemical and process engineering), November 1993, Tokyo, Japan

**INFORMATIC/TELEMATIC** (information technology, telecommunications, automation), July 1993, Bangkok, Thailand

**INTERMACH** (machine tools and metalworking), April 1993, Bangkok, Thailand

**INTERMATEX** (materials handling), June 1993, Harumi, Japan

**INTERNATIONAL DESIGNER** (fashion retail), July 1992, Singapore

**INTERNATIONAL EDUCATION AND TRAINING, LANGUAGE FAIR,** November 1992, Singapore

**INPOCO '93** (pollution control equipment), April 1993, Seoul

**INTERNEPCON KOREA** (electronic components, semiconductors), March 1993, Singapore

**MEASURETECH** (measurement technology), July 1992, Singapore

**PPP MALAYSIA** (printing, packaging, label machinery equipment), October 1993, Kuala Lumpur, Malaysia

**PHARMEX ASIA** (medical technology), June 1994, Bangkok, Thailand

**PRE-PRESS ASIA** (pre-press technology), October 1992, Singapore

**SAFETY AND SECURITY ASIA '93** (safety and security equipment, systems and technology), November 1992, Manila, The Philippines

**SEOUL INSTRUMENT '93** (analytical and scientific instrumentation), December 1992, Seoul

**SINGAPORE INFORMATICS '93** (computers and peripherals), October 1993, Singapore

**SINGAPORE JEWELRY AND WATCH FAIR**, August 1992, Singapore

**TAIPEI AUTO SHOW** (automotive parts and accessories), May 1992, Taipei

**TAIPEI INTERNATIONAL INDUSTRIAL MACHINERY SHOW**, April 1992, Taipei

**TAIPEI INTERNATIONAL MEDICAL EQUIPMENT AND PHARMACEUTICALS SHOW**, November 1992, Taipei

**TECHNOBUILD — KUALA LUMPUR** (building technology), July 1992, Kuala Lumpur, Malaysia

**TECHNOBUILD — BANGKOK** (construction machinery and equipment), September 1992, Bangkok, Thailand

**TELECOMEX/ELECTRONICS ASIA '92** (telecommunications systems and technology and electronics), August 1992, Manila

**THAI TELECOMM** (international telecommunications), August 1992, Bangkok, Thailand

**THAILAND PORT AND MARITIME** (airport and transportation equipment), June 1993, Bangkok, Thailand

**TOYS AND GAMES FAIR**, January 1993, Hong Kong

**TRANSPO ASIA** (cargo and passenger transport), June 1993, Bangkok, Thailand

**WORLD FASHION TRADE FAIR** (apparel), April 1993, Kobe, Japan

# APPENDIX C: PRACTICAL READINGS

Axtell, Roger E., *Do's and Taboos Around the World* (John Wiley & Sons, 1990)

Axtell, Roger E., *Do's and Taboos of Hosting International Visitors* (John Wiley & Sons, 1990)

Axtell, Roger E., *The Do's and Taboos of International Trade* (John Wiley & Sons, 1991)

Business Profile Series [guides on doing business in various countries, including those countries featured in *Doing Business in Asia*] (The Hongkong and Shanghai Banking Corporation Limited)

De Mente, Boye L., *Chinese Etiquette and Ethics in Business* (NTC Business Books, 1989)

De Mente, Boye L., *Korean Etiquette and Ethics in Business* (NTC Business Books, 1988)

Devine, Elizabeth, and Nancy L. Braganti, *The Travelers' Guide to Asian Customs and Manners* (St. Martin's Press, 1986)

Enderlyn, Allyn, and Oliver C. Dziggel, *Cracking the Pacific Rim*, (Probus Publishing, 1992)

Engholm, Christopher, *When Business East Meets Business West* (John Wiley & Sons, 1991)

Fisher, Glen, *International Negotiation* (Intercultural Press, 1980)

*Investor's Guide to the Economic Climate of Singapore* (Singapore International Chamber of Commerce, 1992)

Kato, Hiroki, and Joan Kato, *Understanding and Working with the Japanese Business World* (Prentice-Hall, 1992)

Leppert, Paul A., *How to Do Business With Chinese: Taiwan* (Patton Pacific Press, 1990)

Leppert, Paul A., *Doing Business with the Koreans* (Patton Pacific Press, 1991)

Leppert, Paul A., *Doing Business in Singapore* (Patton Pacific Press, 1990)

Leppert, Paul A., *Doing Business with the Thai* (Patton Pacific Press, 1992)

Moran, Robert T., *Getting Your Yen's Worth* (Gulf Publishing Co., 1985)

Moran, Robert T., and William G. Stripp, *Successful International Business Negotiations* (Gulf Publishing Co., 1991)

Maurer, P. Reed, *Competing in Japan* (The Japan Times, 1989)

Price Waterhouse Information Guide Series [guides on doing business in various countries, including many of the countries featured in *Doing Business in Asia*] (Price Waterhouse)

Rearwin, David, *The Asia Business Book* (Intercultural Press, 1991)

Stross, Randall E., *Bulls in the China Shop* (Pantheon Books, 1990)

*The Economist Guide: Southeast Asia* [also guides for China and Japan (Hutchinson Business Books)

Trade Media Ltd., *Tips for the Business Traveler in Asia* (Probus Publishing, 1992)

*The Wall Street Journal Guides to Business Travel: Pacific Rim* (Fodor's Travel Publications, 1991)

# Index